"This is an important and deepl
would all read with great profit
Suffering from someone who not
but understands the world in w.
worldwide are suffering for their faith as never before. For Western Christians this is a wakeup call – are we prepared to suffer for our faith in a growingly hostile culture? – but it is also profoundly encouraging as we learn of a faithful promise-keeping God who never leaves us or forsakes us, his faithful people."

Bishop Wallace Benn
President of Fellowship of Word and Spirit

"Anyone who has their eyes opened through today's rapid spread of information, to the heart-rending persecution that many in our Christian family are undergoing, and asks 'Why?', needs to get hold of this eminently readable book. It will give you a comprehensive and gripping understanding of the theology behind persecution and encourage you to pray and support more effectively and biblically. I wholeheartedly commend it to you – I couldn't put it down!"

Anne Coles
Head, New Wine Ministry for Women

"Preparing for talks and sermons, planning for a home group study or indeed any moment where we need the biblical foundations to be accurate and grounded – this is where this book comes into its own. Exceptionally helpful, accessible and concise with a clear and logical flow. I commend this book to all church leaders and preachers."

Andy Dipper
Principal and Chief Executive, All Nations Christian College

"On a visit to Pakistan recently I spent time with a woman who had been set on fire because she'd converted from Islam to follow Jesus Christ. Despite the trauma of that horrific experience, Rose shines with the love of Jesus and continues to share God's love with those around her, including those who are still her persecutors. When I asked Rose how she remained so hopeful through so much pain, her joyful reply was, *'because it is perfectly reasonable to expect to find the very best of God in the very worst of circumstances'*.

Rose knows she is persecuted not because she is Rose; but because she follows Jesus Christ. She understands what Jesus meant when he said, *'A servant is not greater than his master. If they persecuted me, they will also persecute you'*, and, *'Blessed are you when people insult you, persecute you and falsely say all kinds of evil against you because of me. Rejoice and be glad, because great is your reward in heaven...'* Remaining hopeful and experiencing joy in difficult or terrible circumstances seems incomprehensible, unless we have a well-developed biblical understanding of suffering and persecution. At Release, our prayer and intention for this book is to help provide that understanding, not just for you but for the millions of our Christian brothers and sisters who are facing real persecution today. Thank you for supporting the mission of Release International by buying this book. Please consider supporting us further, so that you and we can continue doing all we can to love, support, and learn with persecuted Christians worldwide."

Paul Robinson
CEO, Release International

Promise and Persecution

A biblical theology of suffering for Christ

Kenneth Harrod

This book is dedicated to those scholars and pastors, whose writing and teaching on biblical theology have helped me understand better the underlying message of the Bible.

Copyright © 2021 Release International

First edition 2018
Second edition 2021

Published by Release International

ISBN 978-0-9559693-3-1

Kenneth Harrod asserts the moral right to be identified as the author of this work. All rights reserved in all media. No part of this publication may be reproduced, stored in a retrieval system, or transmitted, in any form, or by any means, electronic, mechanical, photocopying, recording or otherwise, without the prior written permission of the author and/or publisher.

Scripture quotations are from The Holy Bible, English Standard Version® (ESV®), copyright © 2001 by Crossway. Used with permission. All rights reserved.

Cover design by Design Chapel

Contents

Foreword by Reverend Canon J. John	7
Preface: A journey of discovery	11

PART ONE: Getting Ready

1.	*Where* do we start?	15
2.	*How* do we start?	19

PART TWO: The Journey

3.	The Promise *made*	33
4.	The Promise *expanded*	45
5.	The Promise *completed*	61
6.	The Promise *fulfilled*	79
7.	The Promise *proclaimed*	97
8.	The Promise *consummated*	119

Conclusion: The discoveries of the journey	133
Appendix: Further reading on biblical theology	143

Foreword

I want to welcome this thoughtful and wise book on the biblical theology of persecution. Any good book on biblical theology is always welcome but one on persecution particularly so. The reason is, quite simply, that we need to talk and think about persecution much more than we do.

Now, in one sense, persecution has been on the agenda for a long time; after all, *Release International*, which is publishing this book, has celebrated its 50th anniversary of working with persecuted Christians. The result is that in church circles we have inevitably heard some of the horrific stories of what's happening to our brothers and sisters in Christ in many parts of the globe. Yet living in a world of information overload and with concerns for so many other things, the plight of the persecuted church is always in danger of being pushed to one side. We need to keep those who suffer for Christ high on our agenda. When we are under orders to love our enemies, it's a pretty poor show if we can't love our family members.

Yet if we need to think about persecution in the context of the global church we also need to think about it in the context of our own culture. It is significant how, in the context of Christianity in the British Isles and other parts of the 'Christian West', the word 'persecution' is creeping into our vocabulary. Oh, to be sure, a lot of it is overstatement: being given a quiet reprimand by your boss for the Christian poster in your office is not quite the same as having your church bulldozed or your pastor thrown into solitary confinement. I do not live in the fear of being arrested simply for being an evangelist. At least, not yet.

Writing such words I am reminded how, when we talk about persecution in countries such as the UK, we are increasingly adding that ominous little postscript: *At least, not yet.*

There have always been pessimistic souls who have taken a gleeful delight in prophesying persecution for the Western Church. What is surely significant is that today, even those of a positive frame of mind are prepared to consider the possibility that things may soon change to the point at which holding to any sort of authentic Christianity is going to be very difficult. The 'Christian Moral Capital' built up over centuries of teaching and preaching has long since been spent and we are badly overdrawn. For some time it has seemed to many Christians that we have shifted from playing a home match to an away game; there is a growing suspicion that the rulebook has been thrown out as well.

In the brave new world of the 21st century we are seeing opposition from various quarters, united only in their contempt and opposition to all that a historic Christianity stands for. So on one side we have the mood of 'political correctness' which demands that we must not make any utterance that could be seen to judge, condemn or make anybody feel, in any way, remotely uncomfortable. And on the other, we have the pressure from other faiths with an agenda to replace Christianity in the public domain. The potential coming together of these two pressures in an unholy alliance against any sort of robust biblical Christianity is troubling.

Now one reason we need to think about persecution is that it is not a simple evil. It is a thing which poses many threats, both obvious and subtle. Let me suggest five threats.

First there is the threat of *dismissal*. Whenever you mention persecution someone will probably casually drop in Tertullian's phrase 'the blood of the martyrs is the seed of the church'. There are two problems with this. One is that it is a glib statement that overlooks the loss and suffering it implies. It is significant that it seems to be rarely said by the persecuted Christians themselves but only by those observing from a safe distance. The other is that it is not true. The 17th century persecution of the Japanese church, memorably and brutally portrayed in Martin Scorsese's *Silence*, effectively ended Christianity in Japan for several centuries. The persecution of the French Huguenots at more or less the same time left behind it empty churches, not full ones. It is neither sensible nor caring to dismiss the threat of persecution.

Second, there is the threat of *danger*. It is perfectly likely that it will soon be very difficult – indeed, in some areas and settings it already is – to share your faith with someone who holds different views, to run a Christian Union, to talk about biblical standards, to wear a cross or to invite people to church without risk of criticism or even legal action. In such an environment the temptation to keep your faith private and secret is going to be irresistible. Sharing your faith is never the easiest of things; even the slightest shadow of persecution is going to make it harder.

The third obvious threat is that of *dilution*. The attacks launched by persecution are rarely against all Christianity, only those forms that hold to those objectionable beliefs such as sin, the deity of Christ, the necessity of having a saving faith and the idea that our allegiance to God ultimately overrules any allegiance to our governments. I have no doubt that our opponents will, in a show of apparent graciousness, allow the existence of an emaciated form of the faith in which we are allowed to respect a bland Jesus who is no more than a good man of history and who neither threatens modern cultural values or dwarfs any other prophets. That watered-down faith will not be the Christianity of the Bible or of history.

A fourth and subtle threat that persecution brings is that of *disillusionment*. The New Testament proclaims the ultimate triumph of Jesus Christ as King of kings and Lord of lords.

Anyone who has seriously read their Bible knows that God's people win in the end. The problem is that many Christians have come to expect that our winning comes sooner rather than later. We may well stand distanced from the prosperity gospel but, nevertheless, there is a feel-good, achievement-filled mood that dominates much of modern Western Christianity. The trouble here is that if you have come to equate the good news as success in this life, then persecution can be seen as a failure of the gospel and of God. If and when persecution breaks out there will no doubt be perplexed cries of 'This isn't supposed to happen!' Well, as this book sensibly reminds us, the idea that God's people will be opposed and persecuted runs throughout the Bible from the very beginning to the very end. As the apostle John writes, 'Do not be surprised, my brothers and sisters, if the world hates you' (1 John 3:13 NIV).

A final threat is *deception*. When the church finds itself under pressure, then there can be the temptation to follow any leader or movement that seems to offer a way out, with no regard for whether or not it is correct. Tough times create a pressure for a deliverer, and some people may not worry too much about what he or she stands for. We need to remember that there's a right reaction to persecution and a wrong one. The most tragic thing that can happen to the church under the pressure of persecution is not that it suffers, but that under the pressure it is warped from being the church of Christ into something very different.

We need to think about, talk about and pray about persecution. Above all we need a firm biblical background, and that is exactly where this book, scholarly and readable, rooted in theology and utterly relevant, is of enormous help. We need to see ourselves in the right perspective; not in terms of the world's big picture but in terms of God's big picture. The Bible reminds us that though we should expect opposition and persecution, we are also assured of God's ultimate victory. **Rev Canon J.John**

Preface:
A Journey of Discovery

THE persecution of Christians has many faces.
In one place it may look like oppressive opposition from the state, leading to arrests, imprisonments and possibly torture.

In another place it may look like the cruel, violent attacks of a religious majority – or, at least, the more extreme elements within that religious majority – resulting in sporadic destruction of property, physical injury and even death.

In other places it may be a worldly love of a particular culture, which grows increasingly intolerant and aggressive as it sees the gospel impacting on, challenging and changing people's lives.

These 'faces', and others like them, can be seen in many places in our world.

Christians in the West live in a culture that has long extolled and valued freedom and people's rights. As such, we have come to assume that *religious* freedom is, and always will be, part of that.

What if that were to change overnight? What if merely attending a Sunday church service suddenly became for us a dangerous exercise? What if running an evangelistic course in someone's home was banned? What if even talking about Christianity to someone who was not a believer could have dire consequences?

What would we do? What would *you* do? Would we have a faith that is big enough to cope with such a reality? For many Christians in our world today, these are not hypothetical questions: they are basic questions that often have to be faced – even by those new to the faith.

Would you turn to God and his word, the Bible? Would you know how to hear God in that word? Would you know how to understand the persecution of Christians – simply for being Christians – from the pages of Scripture? And would you know where to find comfort and reassurance? Would you know how to respond to the sufferings of other Christians?

Promise and Persecution seeks to address these questions. We will go behind the stories – in other words, behind what is happening in our world today – to hear *the* story, the biggest, most important story of all: God's story. To understand God's story is to be better equipped to make sense of the stories around us – and to respond to them as God would want us to.

But as we follow God's story, let's not forget who the author is. That means we read it not to be entertained (as we might read a novel), or just to be informed (as with a reference book) – but to know God *better*.

To know God better should always be our aim, as we seek to listen to and understand the Bible's story – its 'big picture'. To know God better is to be equipped and resourced to serve him, which includes responding, as God would want us to respond, to the world's persecution of his people.

So, where do we begin?

Part One of this book is introductory, and seeks to prepare us to read the big picture of Scripture. *Part Two* then takes us through the Bible's storyline, focusing on some of the major turning points in what we commonly refer to as redemption history. In each of the chapters in *Part Two*, we consider God's promise – as it is expressed at that particular point in the story – and then how conflict, or opposition to God's promise, is seen at that point. Finally, in each chapter, we consider our response to the story so far: in other words, what those elements of the story have shown us that help us understand, and respond to, the persecution of Christians today.

PART ONE

Getting Ready

John 15:18-21

"If the world hates you, know that it has hated me before it hated you. If you were of the world, the world would love you as its own; but because you are not of the world, but I chose you out of the world, therefore the world hates you. Remember the word that I said to you: 'A servant is not greater than his master.' If they persecuted me, they will also persecute you. If they kept my word, they will also keep yours. But all these things they will do to you on account of my name, because they do not know him who sent me."

1. *Where* do we start?

JESUS' words in John 15:18-21, spoken to his disciples the night before the crucifixion, are where many of us might naturally turn first if asked to give a biblical explanation for the persecution of Christians. In these verses we see Jesus stating some important spiritual principles that help us understand the persecution of Christians.

To begin with, it is clear that the world's hatred and persecution of Christians is because *they are identified with Jesus*. The world has hated Jesus. Earlier in John's Gospel, Jesus indicates why: "... it hates me because I testify about it that its works are evil" (John 7:7).

Persecution: a hatred of Jesus

The strong implication behind Jesus' words here in John 15 is that, after his ascension, the world will continue to express that hatred of Jesus in the way it treats his followers. Christians are distinctive (they are "not of the world", as Jesus puts it in verse 19), because they have been chosen by Jesus. For this they will often incite the world's hatred. We might add, then, that the more Christians resemble Jesus in the way they live, and the more they seek to make him known in the world, the more likely it is that they will incur the world's hatred.

Persecution: an ignorance of God

Furthermore, this hatred stems from the world's *ignorance of the one true God*: the world does not know the one who sent Jesus into the world (John 15:21). This makes sense. A true knowledge of God is found only in and through Jesus Christ himself. Earlier that same evening Jesus had declared: "I am the way, and the truth, and the life. No one comes to the Father except through me. If you had known me, you would have known my Father also" (John 14:6-7). And later that evening Jesus would express the implications of that truth in his prayer: "And this is eternal life, that they know you the only true God, and Jesus Christ whom you have sent... I have manifested your name to the people whom you gave me out of the world..." (John 17:3,6). Those who hate Jesus, who reject him, are giving evidence of the fact that they do not know God.

There is much, then, in these verses to help us understand why Christians incur the world's hatred and suffer persecution at the world's hands.[1]

So, how did we get here?

At the risk of stating the obvious, the Bible does not begin with John's Gospel – let alone its 15th chapter! We might well ask how things got to this state of affairs. Why should the world react in this way to Jesus? Indeed, why should it go on reacting to him like this, long after his personal, physical presence in the world has come to an end? Although Jesus' statement doesn't imply that Christians will always be persecuted in the same way and to the same degree, it does clearly warn us that persecution will happen; that it is, to some extent, expected and that we should not be surprised, therefore, when it does happen.

Persecution should not bewilder us or cause us to doubt the truths of our faith. Pastorally, that is important to note, and it is how Jesus ends this part of his teaching that night: "I have said all these things to you to keep you from falling away..." (John 16:1). This was vital, given the foundational role those disciples would have in making known the good news about Jesus. But it

---

[1] For more reflection on these verses, see *Jars of Clay: What the West needs to learn from the persecuted Church*, (Kenneth Harrod, Release International: 2015), pp.35-41

is also so important for every Christian today, whether we happen to live in a part of the world where the church does suffer severe persecution, or whether, as those living in cultures where we take freedom for granted, we are confronted with what is happening to our fellow Christians elsewhere, and want to make sense of it, and want to know how to respond.

Have you ever sat down to watch a TV drama, only to realise you have missed the opening few minutes? Frustrating, isn't it? It can make it so difficult to pick up the threads and understand the significance of what is going on. By the same token, none of us would start to read a novel by opening it half-way through.

On the other hand, when we turn to a dictionary or encyclopaedia for information, we do not feel the need to read everything from page 1!

Perhaps Christians too often approach their Bibles the way they approach a dictionary, dipping in, here and there, as though each book and chapter (and even each verse!) were a stand-alone entity. We need to grasp that the Bible tells a story – not a fictional one, of course, but a story, nonetheless. It tells God's story.

To that end, the next chapter is vital. If the main part of this book is to be thought of as a journey, the next chapter is the map or a set of directions. It shows us how to approach the journey; how to make sense of each landmark. Although, in one sense, the chapter steps back from the specific issue of persecution, don't be put off. It does so to offer a way of reading and understanding the Bible that will, in the long run, help us to understand persecution better, and to see with greater clarity how we in the 21st century should be responding now to the persecution of Christians around the world.

Luke 24:25-27

"And [Jesus] said to them, 'O foolish ones, and slow of heart to believe all that the prophets have spoken! Was it not necessary that the Christ should suffer these things and enter into his glory?' And beginning with Moses and all the Prophets, he interpreted to them in all the Scriptures the things concerning himself."

Luke 24:44-47

"Then [Jesus] said to them, 'These are my words that I spoke to you while I was still with you, that everything written about me in the Law of Moses and the Prophets and the Psalms must be fulfilled.' Then he opened their minds to understand the Scriptures, and said to them, 'Thus it is written, that the Christ should suffer and on the third day rise from the dead, and that repentance and forgiveness of sins should be proclaimed in his name to all nations...'"

2. *How* do we start?

I ONCE saw a fascinating photo on the internet. It showed what looked like a recess of pale coloured rock, possibly on a hillside, with a small, thin, rusting metal rod sticking out of it.

What was interesting for me was the wording that ran alongside it: the photographer had zoomed in on part of the famous Mount Rushmore memorial in the United States (one of George Washington's eyes, to be precise). The description suggested that one of the men who had worked on that incredible piece of sculpture had apparently left a drill-bit stuck in the rock.

Interesting though the image and its description were, it reminded me of a wise comment by a theologian:

> "If one is constantly using the zoom lens on a piece of sculpture such as Mount Rushmore, one will note the worn surface of some rocks and the sedimentary contours of others. But unless one is able to step back with a wide-angle lens and take in 'the big picture', the point of it all has been lost."[2]

How true. Although the photo image I saw was, undoubtedly, fascinating, it's not what Mount Rushmore is really all about. There comes a point when one wants to step back and see the monument in all its glory; to understand and admire the 'big picture'.

---

[2] Stephen G Dempster, *Dominion and Dynasty*, New Studies in Biblical Theology 15 (Nottingham: Apollos, 2003), p.28

Very often in life it is valuable – even necessary – to be able to see the big picture; to be able to step back and understand the shape of the forest rather than just seeing the individual trees. And that is certainly true when it comes to reading, understanding and applying God's word, the Scriptures.

So often, whether we are reading the Bible devotionally on our own, participating in a small-group Bible study or listening to a church sermon, we find ourselves focusing on just a small section of God's word. There's nothing wrong with that, and in many respects it is both practical and inevitable – provided we don't lose sight of the fact that, ultimately, the Bible is *one book*, with a coherent, unifying message.

Despite the fact that the Bible was written by several human authors over a lengthy period of time, and in a variety of literary styles, this important conviction about the Bible's unity is grounded in the belief that the Bible is *God's* word: it is one book with one divine author. The Bible is God's revelation of himself to mankind. But that revelation is embedded in a storyline; one that runs from Creation to the New Creation; one that reveals God's great plan and purpose to redeem a people for himself, to the glory of his name. And, like all storylines, there is *progression*; what appears later builds on what has taken place before. An appreciation of these things should shape the way we read, interpret and apply the Scriptures – *because this is how God has given us his truth.*

The approach that emphasises the need to see the big picture of the Bible, and to interpret the parts in light of the whole, is generally referred to as '**biblical theology**'.

If this approach and emphasis is new to you, I hope that this key preparatory chapter will excite you, and make you want to delve more into God's wonderful word... as well as laying a solid foundation for Part Two, when we return to the issue of persecution.

Reading the big-picture story

So, what is biblical theology? Inevitably, we will scarcely scratch the surface of this topic in one short chapter of a brief book such as this. However, the words of Jesus that introduce this chapter are a good place to start. In two separate incidents – first with two followers on the road to Emmaus, and later in the day with a larger group of disciples – the risen Lord Jesus introduces and illuminates a big-picture reading of Scripture that interprets the parts in the light of the whole. In both incidents he steps back, as it were, to view the whole of Scripture (or, to be more precise: what those disciples would have understood as the whole of Scripture, and what we today call the Old Testament). In doing so, he says, in effect: this is how you should read and understand your Bible!

Let me suggest five principles we can glean from Jesus' words, which give us something of an insight into the strengths and value of a biblical theology approach to reading, understanding and applying the Scriptures.

1. Biblical theology recognises the importance of the 'trajectory' of Scripture

Jesus told his disciples: "... that everything written about me ... must be *fulfilled*"[3] (Luke 24:44). Jesus began his adult ministry sounding a similar note: "Now after John was arrested, Jesus came into Galilee, proclaiming the gospel of God, and saying: 'The time is *fulfilled*, and the kingdom of God is at hand; repent and believe in the gospel'" (Mark 1:14,15). The important New Testament concept of *fulfilment* implies something coming to pass that was promised beforehand; that is, something that was spoken about, hinted at, pointed to or longed for *earlier* in the story. A promise has been made – and now that promise has been kept: it has been *fulfilled*.

---

[3] This and any subsequent use of italics within Bible quotations are the author's own, and are for emphasis.

We have already suggested that God's truth is set before us in the context of a storyline and that, like all stories, it therefore has progression. The very notion of fulfilment encourages us to see a progression in the Scriptures: there is a trajectory that should be respected when we are reading and seeking to apply what we are reading – particularly if we are reading an earlier part of the story.

In other words, the content of the Bible is not 'flat' in the way the content of a telephone directory or a dictionary is – that is, where there is no direct connection or progression in the contents, other than an alphabetical ordering for ease of use. In the case of a dictionary, each entry stands alone, to be dipped into, as we want, where we want, for specific information on a particular subject or word.

Biblical theology's big-picture emphasis reminds us that the Bible is not like that. It encourages us to ask, and to observe, where in the storyline a particular episode or paragraph (or even whole book) occurs – in order to understand its ultimate meaning, in the light of later fulfilment.

2. Biblical theology teaches us to see how all the Scriptures point to Christ and the gospel

A good story leads somewhere; all the twists and turns will ultimately take us to what writers refer to as 'plot resolution'. Every aspect of God's story leads to the salvation he planned and purposed to be fulfilled in his Son, Jesus Christ. The victorious resurrection of Christ is declared in the New Testament to be the "firstfruits" of what will be the final plot resolution. In that context Michael Williams writes:

> "Christ is the centre of the biblical story. Throughout its length, Scripture has a Christ-centred thrust: he will come! The Bible tells the redemptive story of the promised Messiah who came to redeem. That thrust must define our understanding of the nature of Scripture and the way we read it."[4]

---

[4] Michael D Williams, *Far as the Curse is Found* (Phillipsburg: P&R Publishing, 2005), p.14

This is implied in both incidents in Luke 24. When Jesus was with the two men on the road to Emmaus, we read: "And beginning with Moses and all the Prophets, he interpreted to them in all the Scriptures the things concerning himself" (Luke 24:27).

The second incident brings out this point even more strongly. "Then he said to them, 'These are my words that I spoke to you while I was still with you, that everything written about me in the Law of Moses and the Prophets and the Psalms must be fulfilled'" (Luke 24:44).

The Hebrew Scriptures contain the same books that we find in our Old Testament, but there are some differences in terms of the order in which they appear. In the Hebrew canon the books are divided into three groups: the law, the prophets and the writings. The book of Psalms heads the third group. Jesus' statement, then, appears to be a way of emphasising that the Scriptures, *in their entirety*, point to, and find their fulfilment, in him.

Indeed, as if to emphasise this point, Luke continues: "Then he opened their minds to understand the Scriptures, and said to them, '*Thus it is written*, that the Christ should suffer and on the third day rise from the dead, and that repentance and forgiveness of sins should be proclaimed in his name to all nations, beginning from Jerusalem'" (Luke 24:45-47).

"Thus it is written," says Jesus; and yet, we will search in vain for a single 'written' verse in the Old Testament that says explicitly what Jesus goes on to say - in the way that he says it: namely, that the promised Messiah/Christ should *suffer* and on the third day rise again, and that forgiveness of sins would be proclaimed in his name to all nations.

Frequently, of course, we *do* see Jesus and the New Testament writers quoting or clearly paraphrasing individual verses from the Old Testament Scriptures, but here Jesus seems to be doing something subtly different. It's as if he is saying to his disciples: "This is what, at the end of the day, the Scriptures *as a whole* are saying; this is what the storyline is pointing to; this is the big picture, the big message." And that message is the gospel: that Jesus, who is the promised Messiah, had to suffer and die on the cross in our place, on our behalf and for our sins; that he would rise again as victor over sin and death, and that his finished atoning work requires of us a response of repentance and faith, if we might benefit from that work on the cross in the forgiveness of our sins.

Biblical theology aligns our reading of the Scriptures with the gospel.

3. Biblical theology enables us to preach truly Christian sermons from the Old Testament

In a sense this follows from the previous point. Christians, and that includes some Christian preachers, will sometimes struggle to know what to *do* with the Old Testament, or at least with some parts of it. How do we present a pertinent message for today? We have no trouble talking about Christ and making some contemporary application if we're looking at Isaiah 53, but what about some of the historical sections? Or some of the seemingly obscure laws?

In an attempt to be faithful to the Bible as God's word – and to make the whole of the Bible relevant to us today – one solution to this dilemma that many readers of the Bible adopt is an application and message that we might refer to as 'moralism'. "Such-and-such a Bible character did this (which is good), so we should also do this..."; "Such-and-such a Bible character did that (which is bad), so we shouldn't do that..." That is a caricature, granted, but I hope you see the point. The basic mistake being made here is to want to jump directly from the Old Testament episode to today, to *me*, as if application of the Bible is about drawing a straight line, direct from any part of the Bible to my life, with a neat, self-contained message for today. Such an approach to reading and applying the Bible is understandable (particularly as it tends to spring from the good and faithful conviction that the Bible is God's *living*, relevant word). However, it bypasses, and fails to recognise, the manner, shape and way in which God has given us that word. And because it fails to do so, it runs the risk of making direct applications to our lives today that are not warranted by the original text of Scripture.

Many examples of this could be given. One of the more famous is the Sunday school favourite: David and Goliath (1 Samuel 17). An approach that ignores where it is set in the biblical story and, rather, simply draws a straight line from text to today might yield a message along the lines of "our faith overcomes our enemies". After all, David declares to Goliath that he comes before him "in the name of the Lord of hosts" (verse 45), and that "the battle is the Lord's" (verse 47). So, it is said, we need a strong faith like David's to overcome *our* enemies. An even worse development is one which tries to equate David's "five smooth stones" (verse 40) with those things that aid our faith (Bible reading, prayer, Christian fellowship, and so on).

Biblical theology challenges us to approach the application of the Bible somewhat differently; to see where in the overall storyline an episode occurs (as this helps us understand its original intent and meaning) and then to observe the trajectory of Scripture to see how that original meaning finds its fulfilment in the light of Christ and the gospel.

In other words, we would start by asking what a particular verse or passage *means*. Not "What does this passage say *to me?*", as if I should extract some mystical meaning for myself today that ignores its original context and setting, but what did the author, inspired by God, intend to convey, and how would it have been received by his original readers? As James Hamilton puts it:

> "One of the primary aims of biblical theology is to understand and embrace the worldview of the biblical authors. In order to do this, we have to know the

story they take for granted, the connections they see between the events in that story, and the ways they read later parts of the story by the light that emanates from its earlier parts."[5]

This original meaning – that gives due consideration for where in the storyline the passage occurs – can then be traced along the trajectory line of Scripture until we see that meaning being fulfilled in its New Testament context. This is not about arbitrarily finding Christ in every verse of the Bible without any control or principle: it is about respecting the form in which God has given his revelation to us.

So, to go back to our example of David and Goliath: this famous story occurs in 1 Samuel 17. In the previous chapter David is anointed by Samuel to be king. David is not just one of the people of Israel; he is God's chosen one, on whom the Spirit has come (1 Samuel 16:13). We need to read his encounter with Goliath in that light before pursuing a message for today. If we can identify with anyone in the story it is the people of Israel, who are unable to conquer the enemy. But where the people are helpless, the anointed king goes out, seemingly against all the odds and from what appears to be a position of human weakness, and conquers the enemy. Only then are the people able to share in the victory won for them by the king (verse 52). When the story is seen in that light – of the victory of the one anointed to be king – it should be obvious that we track the storyline to Jesus' victory – rather than to *our* faith.

This is not allegory (that medieval method of reading our doctrine *back* into the Old Testament); this is typology: taking the historical story at face value, and looking for what type of fulfilment emerges later in the storyline of the Bible.

---

[5] James M Hamilton Jr, *What is Biblical Theology?* (Wheaton: Crossway, 2014), p.12

4. Biblical theology lets the Bible set the agenda for how the Bible should be read

This, in a sense, is where the previous three principles are taking us. It is, I would argue, a fundamental, Spirit-prompted Christian conviction in us that the Bible is the word of God. But when we begin reading and studying it, the Bible doesn't look like a doctrinal statement of faith or a set of commandments (although it contains examples of both!) – or even a gospel tract. It looks like an epic story. Its shape, its direction, its promises, its mini-resolutions and its ultimate resolution all contribute to its divine purpose – and so all play a part in our understanding of, and our application of, what we read.

Biblical theology is not just 'theology that is biblical' (although it should certainly be *at least* that, in the sense that we want our theology to be derived from the Bible!). It is also an approach that respects that shape, direction and purpose that we find when we look at the Scriptures themselves.

It has often been said that the overall shape of the Bible's storyline can be summed up in four parts:

Creation ⇨ Fall ⇨ Redemption ⇨ New Creation

That is a helpful summary – and so is the recognition and acknowledgement of where *we* are in that storyline. This will hopefully be evident as we work through the Bible's story, and as we seek to apply this big-picture view of Scripture to the issue of persecution.

To say that biblical theology lets the Bible set the agenda for how the Bible should be read is to affirm that biblical theology is, in essence, a practical theology that benefits us all.

Many Christians will be familiar with works of systematic theology, which summarise the content of the Christian faith. Knowing, for example, what is true about God and about Christ, what we should believe for salvation, the nature and purpose of the church, and the end of all things are important matters. Christianity has content. *Systematic* theology, as the name suggests, seeks to sum up those things for us, in an ordered, presentable way. Systematic theology asks: "What does the Bible say about...?" Its fruit is doctrine, what we believe.

Biblical theology, however, logically *precedes* the work of systematics, for we need tools that enable us to interpret the Bible appropriately and biblically before we can do that work of summing up and ordering what the Bible says about particular themes or topics.

We might sum up what we have been saying like this:

Exegesis ⇨ **Biblical theology** ⇨ Systematics
(what does it mean?) (what do we believe?)

'Exegesis' is simply the word Christians use to refer to that preliminary question of asking what a passage *means*: what the author intended, and how his original hearers would have understood what he said. Biblical theology then guides us along the trajectory of Scripture to see what that original meaning looks like today, in the light of Christ and the gospel. Biblical theology enables us to knit the story together, to understand the parts in the light of the whole. And if you value your Bible, and consider it the word of God, that is exciting! As Michael Lawrence enthusiastically puts it:

> "Biblical theology is practical theology, because it gives us the whole Bible to use as God intended it: gospel-centred, Christ-exalting, life-transforming Scripture. It doesn't get any more practical, any more useful than that."[6]

5. Biblical theology sums up how Jesus taught his disciples to read Scripture

This, finally, is the 'clincher' and takes us back to where this

---

[6] Michael Lawrence, *Biblical Theology in the life of the church* (Wheaton: Crossway, 2010), p.83

chapter began: with the words of the risen Lord Jesus to his disciples. Jesus teaches that the whole promise-laden storyline of the Old Testament Scriptures finds its meaning, its purpose, its fulfilment, in *him*.

As we then read on into the pages of the New Testament, we find the apostles applying those principles, as they preach sermons and as they write letters to churches and church leaders. In the Gospels, the disciples are often depicted as being slow to understand what Jesus was teaching. After the resurrection and ascension of Jesus things were very different. Inspired by the Holy Spirit, they see their original Scriptures – our Old Testament – in a new light: in a Christ-centred light. They see how the story has been unfolding, and how promise – and hope – is realised in Jesus.

This, then, has been our brief peek at the exciting world of biblical theology. I began this chapter by saying we could barely scratch the surface – given that this chapter is intended to prepare us for the journey that follows; one that will help us understand, and know how to respond to, the persecution of Christians for their faith in Christ.

If, however, as a result of reading this chapter, you want to explore more of the exciting, important – and practical – world of biblical theology, the short Appendix to this book offers suggestions for further reading.

Graeme Goldsworthy provides a memorable summary of the principles we have been observing in this chapter:

> "Biblical theology is nothing more nor less than allowing the Bible to speak as a whole: as the one word of the one God about the one way of salvation."[7]

In Part Two of this book, we will bring the discipline of biblical theology, and a biblical theology reading of Scripture, to

---

[7] Graeme Goldsworthy, *Preaching the whole Bible as Christian Scripture* (Leicester: IVP, 2000), p.7

bear upon the issue of persecution. To do so, we will pick up one significant theme within the storyline of Scripture: that of *promise*.

PART TWO

The Journey

Genesis 3:14,15

"The Lord God said to the serpent,
'Because you have done this,
    Cursed are you above all livestock
    and above all beasts of the field;
on your belly you shall go,
    and dust you shall eat
    all the days of your life.
I will put enmity between you and the woman,
    and between your offspring and her offspring;
he shall bruise your head,
    and you shall bruise his heel."

3. The Promise *made*

WE have suggested in the previous chapter that biblical theology is a vital tool for every Christian, for it enables us to read the Bible in the way the Bible itself suggests we should be reading it. It allows us to hear clearly what each part of the Bible would say to us today, by understanding where each part comes in God's storyline.

But now we need to return to our main theme: the persecution of God's people. Our aim in this central part of the book is to bring that discipline of biblical theology and a biblical theology reading of Scripture to bear on the issue of persecution. This is no mere theoretical exercise. Our desire is two-fold: first, to have a better biblical grasp of persecution and, second, to allow this big-picture reading of Scripture to shape our response to persecution. A solid, biblical understanding should lead to a godly, biblical response on our part.

In summarising what biblical theology is and its implications for our reading and interpreting of Scripture, we have referred to the way God's revelation to mankind is embedded in a storyline. All storylines have a natural progression, with later elements building on earlier ones. Moreover, it is assumed that we will notice and understand those earlier elements. This enables us to recognise the way later parts of the story build on what has gone before.

We have referred to that progression in the Bible's storyline as a 'trajectory': an ascending path, if you like, as God fills out more and more of the picture, moving us towards the climax of his great plan and purpose for all of creation.

As you will see from the headings for all the chapters that follow, we are going to follow the theme of *promise* along that trajectory of Scripture – and learn how it can help us understand the persecution of Christians today.

All good storylines will have key, pivotal moments. These will be events that develop the central story. In a work of fiction these pivotal moments are often what keep us reading.

The Bible's storyline has certain key moments that take God's purposes on to the next stage. Theologians will sometimes refer to the various 'epochs' of the Bible, and sometimes point to the various expressions of 'covenant', as ways of describing these pivotal events in the story. That's what we will be doing with the concept of God's promise.

PROMISE IN JUDGEMENT

We begin at the beginning! The verses at the start of this chapter constitute the first promise in the Bible. Ironically, it is a promise embedded in a word of judgement.

Following the disastrous and cataclysmic act by the man and woman to disobey his word, the Lord God speaks words of judgement, first to the serpent (Genesis 3:14-15), and then to the woman and man (Genesis 3:16-19). But it is the very words of judgement upon the serpent that contain a glimpse of hope, indeed of promise, for the man and woman.

The first 'good news'

Earlier, in Genesis 2:17, God had warned the man and woman that, if they ate of the tree of the knowledge of good and evil, they would "surely die". Having done so, Adam and Eve might naturally have assumed, therefore, that as God now calls them out of hiding (Genesis 3:8-11) their time has come. Mankind will be extinguished! The Lord, however, turns first to the serpent, and speaks words of judgement to him; and it is in those very words that the man and the woman would have heard a signal of hope. For the *promise* within the judgement of verse 15 implies the story will not end at this point. The verse implies there *is* a future for mankind.

For this reason, Genesis 3:15 has often been referred to as the Bible's *protoevangelium* – literally, the first good news, or at least the first glimmer of good news. But it is only a glimmer, a small shaft of light in the darkness. It talks of enmity between the seed of the woman and the seed of the serpent, and it gently, subtly implies a victory for the seed of the woman (on the basis that a bruising of the head is more serious than a bruising of the heel). Nevertheless, Genesis 3:15 does not state the gospel in the way you or I would state the gospel today. That's because it is only the beginning of the story. As James Hamilton eloquently puts it:

> "As an acorn grows into an oak tree, Genesis 3:15 grows into the good news of Jesus Christ."[8]

In the immediate context of Genesis 3, we might well ask who is the serpent and who is (or are) the respective offspring being referred to. Most of us would instinctively read 'Satan' for serpent in this passage; partly perhaps because the serpent clearly stands opposed to God in the Eden story, but more probably because imagery later in the Bible (eg Revelation 12:9, 20:2) leads us to this conclusion. In the latter case (whether we realise it or not), we are allowing a biblical theology reading of the Bible's storyline to inform our understanding of what we are reading in Genesis 3!

But what of the seed (or "offspring" as English translations tend to render that word)? Intriguingly, the Hebrew word for seed never occurs in a plural form in the Old Testament.[9] Rather

---

[8] Hamilton, *What is Biblical Theology?* p.12
[9] I am indebted to Hamilton for this observation. See 'The Skull-Crushing Seed of the Woman: Inner-Biblical Interpretation of Genesis 3:15', *The Southern Baptist Journal of Theology 10, number 2,* 2006, p.32

like the English word 'sheep', the singular form serves to refer to both single and plural. This potential ambiguity will be important as the story unfolds.

The second phrase in Genesis 3:15 might imply the collective offspring of both the woman and of the serpent. The last part of the verse, however, seems to refer explicitly to an individual: "*He* shall bruise your head..." This tension between the many and the one, between the collective group and an individual representative, will become a significant feature of the Bible's storyline, as God's great plan and purpose unfold. The prophet Isaiah's depiction of the 'Servant' is a good example of this. At times it seems the nation is being referred to (Isaiah 41:8; 44:1), while at other times it seems an individual is in view (Isaiah 42:1; 52:13).

This tension is reinforced by observing that there is not an exact parallel between the different parts of Genesis 3:15. God begins by saying he will put enmity between 'you' (the serpent) and 'the woman'. He then adds: "... and between your [the serpent's] offspring and her [the woman's] offspring..." But in the final part of the verse, the Lord says that 'he' [the offspring/seed of the woman] shall bruise not 'his', or even 'their' [the offspring/seed of serpent's] head - as we might have expected at that point - but rather 'your' head [the serpent himself]. The ongoing enmity will be between the seed of the woman and the seed of the serpent - and yet the decisive action will concern the seed of the woman and the serpent himself!

THE ORIGIN OF CONFLICT

If Genesis 3:15 is a *protoevangelium* - a first promise of the gospel - we need to recognise that it is also a *protoantithesis* - the first sign of **conflict**. Specifically, as we shall see, here is the beginning of a historical conflict that will issue forth in hostility towards God's people: that is to say, persecution. As Michael Williams puts it:

> "From this point forward, two opposing forces war in the world: the kingdom of God and the kingdom of Satan, the kingdom of light and the kingdom of darkness, the seed of the woman and the seed of the serpent... Due to the sin in the Garden, two kingdoms stand antithetically to one another, a contention that will pit God against all that is in opposition to his rule... Human beings, the seed spoken of in Genesis 3:15, are either the friends of God or the enemies of God."[10]

After the completion of the Garden of Eden narrative, the next story is that of the murder of Abel by his brother, Cain (Genesis 4:1-16). The episode begins with both men apparently seeking to approach the Lord:

> "In the course of time Cain brought to the Lord an offering of the fruit of the ground, and Abel also brought of the firstfruit of his flock and of their fat portions. And the Lord had regard for Abel and his offering, but for Cain and his offering he had no regard." (Genesis 4:3-5)

Christians have often speculated on what exactly made Cain's offering unacceptable. Was it that he only offered leftover fruit and veg (rather than the best)? Or was it because it was not a blood sacrifice in the way Abel's had been?

There may be some truth in either – or both – suggestions. But such speculation, I believe, misses the big-picture point, to some extent. Here we are seeing the first outworking of God's promise in Genesis 3:15: those who are the seed of the woman and those who are the seed of the serpent are revealing (and, therefore, distinguishing) themselves by their actions. Cain, who

---

[10] Michael D Williams, *Far as the Curse is Found*, p.69

is not accepted by God, attacks and kills Abel, who is. On what basis do we say that? A biblical-theological, big-picture view of Scripture! Much later in the storyline, the apostle John writes about the love that should exist between those who are God's people, at which point he adds this telling comment:

> "We should not be like Cain, *who was of the evil one* and murdered his brother. And why did he murder him? Because his own deeds were evil and his brother's righteous." (1 John 3:12)

Do you see what John is doing? He is tracing that theme of conflict along the trajectory of God's revelation. The story of Cain's murder of Abel is not just a gruesome, individual instance of fratricide in ancient times; it is far more significant than that (that's why it's in the Bible, after all). It marks the beginning of a cosmic struggle, in which the seed of the serpent opposes the seed of the woman. Often, as in this case, it will do so violently.

John's identifying of Cain with the seed of the serpent is supported by the content of the original story itself. The Lord's response to Cain's evil act is to declare: "And now you are cursed..." (Genesis 4:11). Although English translations tend to obscure this, the Hebrew phrase is identical to the Lord's words to the serpent: "Cursed are you..." (Genesis 3:14). It is as though the original readers were meant to think of the serpent from Chapter 3 when they read of Cain in Chapter 4.[11] Similarly, at the end of the episode, Eve conceives and gives birth to Seth, and declares: "God has appointed for me another offspring (seed) instead of Abel..." (Genesis 4:25). The point here would seem to be not merely that the Lord has provided numerical compensation for a grieving mother – but he has ensured the continuation of the seed of the woman.

---

[11] Of course, chapter divisions were not part of the original Scriptures.

Two lines of people (Genesis 4-11)

Again, we can see we are on the right lines here by observing how the story unfolds. The rest of Genesis chapters 4-11[12] are characterised and dominated by observing these two lines of people: those who are God's people and those who are not; in other words, those who are the seed of the woman and those who are the seed of the serpent. The genealogies that appear in these chapters reinforce this and help sustain hope in the promise of God. As if to illustrate this, in the genealogy of Seth (the godly line), we read:

> "When Lamech had lived 182 years, he fathered a son and called his name Noah, saying, 'Out of the ground that the Lord *has cursed* this one shall bring us relief from our work and from the painful toil of our hands.'" (Genesis 5:28-29)

The reference to God's words of judgement in the Garden is unmistakable. For the original readers this would have served as a reminder of the promise of Genesis 3:15, and kept alive the hope that one day there would appear a seed of the woman through whom that promise would be fulfilled. But although, after the Flood, God does indeed make a fresh start with Noah (compare Genesis 9:1-2 with Genesis 1:28), the story and the conflict doesn't end with him: the conflict between the two lines quickly resumes and continues.

And so it *will* continue. As we follow the development of God's promise, we will see the continuation of this conflict between the two seeds. The creative tension between the corporate and singular will also continue – as will the hope and expectation that one day an individual seed of the woman *will* appear and will triumph over the serpent and his seed.

---

[12] The first 11 chapters of Genesis are generally recognised as a unit, sometimes referred to as 'pre-history'.

Ultimately, this will point us to Jesus. He is the *singular* seed of the woman, who conquers the serpent, but who suffers in doing so. All who belong to him constitute the *corporate* seed of the woman, and will find themselves caught up in this conflict.

This brings us back to the apostle John's understanding of the Cain and Abel story in his first letter. We saw how John identified Cain as the representative seed of the serpent (1 John 3:12). In the very next verse, John writes: "Do not be surprised, brothers, that the world hates you" (1 John 3:13). Where have we already heard that? John's words are a clear paraphrasing, or referencing, of the teaching Jesus gave the night before he was crucified, in the verses we referred to in Part One (John 15:18). We might ask what it is that takes John from talking about love among Christians (1 John 3:11) to the example of Cain (who didn't love his brother: 1 John 3:12) to a reference to the way the *world* treats Christians. Where is the logic in that? Our biblical-theological, big-picture reading of Scripture helps us again here.

The apostle John would have been among those privileged to hear the lectures in biblical theology that Jesus gave after his resurrection (Luke 24). John knows how to make the connections across the storyline of Scripture. He impresses on his readers the need for Christians to love one another, for this is evidence that they are "of God" (1 John 3:10). By contrast, a hatred of Christians is evidence that someone is a seed of the serpent, in the way Cain, who murdered his righteous brother, was a seed of the serpent. It is quite logical, therefore, for John then to recall what Jesus had said at the Last Supper about the world's attitude to the disciples. It was John who, earlier in his Gospel account, records Jesus telling his opponents that by their actions they were demonstrating that they were "of your father the devil" (John 8:44). In other words, those who oppose Jesus were and are the (collective) seed of the serpent. So when, as he warns them in John 15, the world hates Jesus' followers, it is demonstrating that, in big-picture terms, it is the seed of the serpent, just as Cain's actions did.

OUR RESPONSE TO THE STORY SO FAR

" 'I will put enmity between you and the woman, and between your offspring and her offspring...' said the Lord to the serpent" (Genesis 3:15a). What does this conflict look like, at least on the surface?

Here's what it looks like: Cain murders Abel. Esau hates Jacob, who is forced to flee. Pharaoh destroys a generation. Saul pursues David. The Jews and Gentiles conspire to have Jesus executed. And Jesus warns his disciples that the world will treat his followers the way it responded to him.

In other words, as each new chapter of the Bible's storyline opens, it *appears* that the seed of the serpent has the upper hand. He seems stronger. It looks like he will secure the victory. Evil will win.

And isn't that what it sometimes feels like when we face the reality of Christians being persecuted today? When we read of pastors and preachers being imprisoned? When we read of Christian communities being attacked and slaughtered? In the midst of harrowing stories of suffering from around the world, it seems that evil triumphs. The seed of the serpent conquers. Persecution feels like Christianity being defeated – eradicated.

But contrary to appearances, the Bible shows us that God remains sovereign over all things and circumstances, and therefore his plan and purpose will not be thwarted. And so, to remind us of this and to encourage us, we see in that same biblical storyline that the godly line is maintained through Seth. Jacob, the chosen one, is protected. The Lord preserves Moses and uses him to effect salvation for his people. God thwarts Saul and establishes David's kingdom.

And God raises Jesus from the dead.

Above all, the resurrection of Jesus Christ proclaims his victory over sin, death – and evil. On the eve of his crucifixion, Jesus declared: "Now is the judgement of this world; now will the ruler of this world be cast out" (John 12:31). Jesus' atoning death on the cross not only meant the cancelling of the record of debt that stood against us as sinners, but it also constituted a disarming of and a triumphing over the spiritual powers of evil (Colossians 2:14-15). In that passage from John's first letter that we have referred to, John declares:

> "The reason the Son of God appeared was to destroy the works of the devil." (1 John 3:8)

Jesus Christ is the one who fulfils the promise-in-judgement of Genesis 3:15. He is the individual seed of the woman who defeats the serpent and his seed. A biblical-theological, big-picture reading of the Bible's storyline encourages us to look beyond what is on the surface and before our eyes, in order to perceive the ultimate reality of history.

See the victory

From this first chapter of the story alone – especially as we learn to trace its themes along the trajectory of Scripture – we should recognise the spiritual root behind everything that leads to the persecution of Christians. We live in what the New Testament describes as "the present evil age" (Galatians 1:4) and the Bible tells us: "We do not wrestle against flesh and blood, but against the rulers, against the authorities, against the cosmic powers over this present darkness, against the spiritual forces of evil…" (Ephesians 6:12). That should inform our understanding of persecution and, importantly, it should begin to shape our priorities, in terms of how we respond to what is happening around the world.

At the same time, the foundational nature of Genesis 3:15 establishes not only the basis for understanding the conflict that will bring about persecution, it also declares the promise that Jesus Christ has the final and certain victory over the serpent. In that certainty we are to live. And in that certainty we are to encourage all of God's people to live.

Genesis 12:1-3

"Now the Lord said to Abram, 'Go from your country and your kindred and your father's house to the land that I will show you. And I will make of you a great nation, and I will bless you and make your name great, so that you will be a blessing. I will bless those who bless you, and him who dishonours you I will curse, and in you all the families of the earth shall be blessed."

4. The Promise *expanded*

BY anyone's reckoning, Genesis 12 constitutes a major turning point in the Bible's story. The previous chapters have painted broad brushstrokes across the generations. Various genealogies have kept the story moving at a considerable pace. Now it all slows down. The remaining 39 chapters in the book of Genesis will concentrate on just four generations of one family: Abraham, Isaac, Jacob and Jacob's twelve sons.

And yet there *is* continuity with what has gone before. Abraham (or Abram, as he was originally known) first appears at the end of chapter 11, as part of yet another genealogy. In particular, he is identified as being from the (godly) line of Shem, whose genealogy comes directly after the Tower of Babel incident (Genesis 11:1-9). The people who had gathered in the land of Shinar declare: "Come, let us build ourselves a city and a tower with its top in the heavens, and let us make a name for ourselves, lest we be dispersed over the face of the whole earth" (Genesis 11:4).

At first glance, we might well assume this was perfectly innocent. And yet the way the Lord responds to this (Genesis 11:5-9) clearly suggests that what they were doing was wrong. If we view the incident in the light of God's original purpose for creation (if we respect the big-picture, in other words), the significance becomes more apparent. Theirs was, it would seem, an attempt to live life without reference to the one true God; to 'make a name for themselves'. God is, to all intents and purposes, redundant – even irrelevant. But that is rebellion. That is the collective seed of the serpent showing its true colours.

Intriguingly, and as if to emphasise these two lines of people we have been referring to, 'Shem' means 'name'. Graeme Goldsworthy comments,

> "... the godless race seeks for its *shem* by its own efforts (Genesis 11:4) only to be frustrated by the judgement of God. This contrasts with the godly line of Shem which shows that we can achieve a name only as the objects of God's saving grace; that the only renown that counts is to be known as the people of God who are called by his name."[13]

It has often been pointed out that, throughout Genesis chapters 4 to 11, each act of divine judgement is followed by an expression of divine grace. But where is the divine grace after the dispersing of people in Genesis 11? Robert L. Reymond responds:

> "Does not God's call of Abraham in Genesis 12, in whom all the dispersed nations of the earth would be blessed, answer to the character of the Babel judgement and thus complete the judgement/grace pattern? It would seem so."[14]

Here, then, is the context for the calling of Abraham. By God's grace, he is of the godly line; he is part of the collective seed of the woman. And it is through him that God's story will now progress.

GOD'S PROMISE BEING EXPANDED

The opening verses of Genesis 12 present an expansion on, or development of, God's promise. In our previous chapter we saw

---

[13] Graeme Goldsworthy, *According to Plan: The Unfolding Revelation of God in the Bible* (Leicester: IVP, 1991), p.150
[14] Robert L. Reymond, *A New Systematic Theology of the Christian Faith*, 2nd Edition (Nashville; Thomas Nelson, 2001), p.118

how, at the birth of Noah, hope was expressed in terms of the promise-in-judgement within the verses of Genesis 3. Now God makes specific promises to Abraham: to make of him a nation, to bless him and to make him the source of blessing to others. References to 'bless' or 'blessing' occur no fewer than five times in the space of these three verses. God's promise will be bound up with God's blessing.

"... In you all the families of the earth shall be blessed," says the Lord at the end of the paragraph (Genesis 12:3). That sounds like quite a promise – and it is! But where is it leading? How do we hear, read and apply that promise today?

The blessing of the nations

A biblical theology reading of Scripture requires us to trace this promise into the New Testament. In his letter to the Galatians, the apostle Paul writes:

> "Know then that it is those of faith who are the sons of Abraham. And the Scripture, foreseeing that God would justify the Gentiles by faith, *preached the gospel* beforehand to Abraham, saying, 'In you shall all the nations be blessed.' So then, those who are of faith are blessed along with Abraham, the man of faith."
> (Galatians 3:7-9)

Paul refers to the promise of Genesis 12:3 as the gospel! And yet, as we also noted with Genesis 3:15, so we might observe that Genesis 12:1-3 says nothing explicitly about Jesus Christ, the cross, the empty tomb, atonement or God's means of forgiving our sins. So how can Paul refer to these verses as "the gospel"? What is Paul doing? He is doing biblical theology! He is reading the Bible in the way Jesus taught us to read the Bible. He is picking up the significant promise of God – that he will bless all kinds of people through one specific, chosen, representative person – and he is tracing that theme along the trajectory of the

Bible's storyline. And that leads, inexorably, to Jesus. In referring to Genesis 12:3 as "the gospel", then, Paul is saying that this promise of God, given originally to the patriarch Abraham, anticipates the gospel; it is part of the trajectory of promise that is leading to Jesus Christ. If we follow Paul's lead (which is another way of saying if we allow the Bible to teach us how to read and apply the Bible!), we cannot properly read or preach from Genesis 12:1-3 without focusing on how *Jesus* blesses all peoples by dying for us on the cross.

So what does it mean to be blessed by God? Often we think and speak of this concept in immediate, this-life terms: "The Lord really blessed me today..." While it is right to acknowledge God's goodness working in our day-to-day lives (and to thank him for it!), the Lord's *blessing us* is ultimately about *relationship*. Psalm 32:1-2 reminds us:

> "Blessed is the one whose transgression is forgiven,
>   whose sin is covered.
> Blessed is the man against whom the Lord counts no iniquity."

In his letter to the Romans, Paul quotes these verses as the flipside of what it means to be justified by grace, through faith (see Romans 4:1-8). To be justified before God is to be counted as righteous (because of Christ's righteousness) – which means *not* to have our iniquities counted against us. Blessing concerns our relationship with God. Mary J Evans sums this up well:

> "New Testament teaching echoes the Old Testament view of blessing and cursing as relational. The ultimate and only important blessing is that of belonging to God, being part of his people, a member of his family. The only real curse is being out of relationship with God, outside of the community of blessing. In temporal contexts both blessings and

curses can be described in material terms, but their material dimension is secondary. Although bad things can and do happen to those who belong to the kingdom, those who are part of God's people cannot be under the curse; rather they are blessed."[15]

From Abraham to David

It is perhaps worth stressing at this point that there is nothing arbitrary or novel about Paul's referencing of Genesis 12:3, and its development within the Bible's storyline. This significant promise to Abraham is repeated to Isaac (Genesis 26:4) and then to Jacob (Genesis 28:14). As that Bible storyline continues to unfold, this representative who will bring blessing to others, this individual seed of the woman, will eventually be identified as a son of David (more of which in the next chapter) – and, again, the promise of Genesis 12:3 is identified with him (see Psalm 72:17).

At the beginning of Luke's Gospel, both Mary and Zechariah acknowledge this link in the storyline between Abraham and David. Mary, who had been told that her child would receive "the throne of his father *David*" (Luke 1:32), then praises God for remembering his mercy "as he spoke to our fathers, to *Abraham* and to his offspring [seed] forever" (Luke 1:54-55). Similarly, John the Baptist's father, Zechariah, praises God for raising up salvation in *David's* house, but states that this is "to remember his holy covenant, the oath that he swore to our father *Abraham*..." (Luke 1:72-73). Robert L Reymond comments on the declarations of Mary and Zechariah:

"...whereas Christians today mainly only celebrate the Incarnation of God's Son at Christmas time, Mary and Zechariah, placing this event in its covenant

---

[15] M J Evans, 'Blessing/Curse' in *New Dictionary of Biblical Theology*, Eds: T Desmond Alexander & Brian S Rosner (Leicester: IVP, 2000), p.401

context, saw reason in his coming to celebrate the *covenant faithfulness* of God to his people. In their awareness of the broader significance of the event and the words of praise which that awareness evoked from them we see biblical theology at its best being worked out and expressed!"[16]

As one final example, we see the apostle Peter, preaching a Christ-centred, gospel message to his fellow Jews in Jerusalem – and urging them to recognise that the covenant promise *made to Abraham* has been fulfilled in Jesus. Peter declares: "You are the sons of the prophets and of the covenant that God made with your fathers, saying to Abraham, 'And in your offspring shall all the families of the earth be blessed'" (Acts 3:25). Peter is quoting from Genesis 22:18 which is itself a development on the original form of the promise given to Abraham in Genesis 12:3 – in that it is now through Abraham's offspring (seed) that the families of the earth will be blessed.

CONFLICT IN THE MIDST OF PROMISE

But we are still trying to understand persecution! So, if we go back to Genesis 12, what we must also notice is that in the middle of all that promise of blessing, **conflict** is still present! "I will bless those who bless you, and *him who dishonours you I will curse,*" says the Lord. Although God is going to bless Abraham, there will be those who oppose him. And because God is going to bless Abraham (and, perhaps more significantly, make him a source of blessing to others), those who *do* oppose him will be cursed by God. Cursed, as the serpent was cursed. This perspective helps us understand so much of the Old Testament storyline, not least the hugely significant sequence of events we refer to as the Exodus.

---

[16] Robert L Reymond, *A New Systematic Theology of the Christian Faith*, p.516

The Exodus salvation

The story of the patriarchs is, in many ways, the story of God preserving the seed of the woman, the line through which God is going to bless all peoples. By the end of the book of Genesis, however, Jacob's family are not in the land they were promised; they are in Egypt. As we turn the page into the book of Exodus, we quickly discover them facing hardship and hostility. They are persecuted. Enmity is personified in Pharaoh, who attempts to slaughter a generation of male children – the seed of the serpent attempting to cut off the line of the seed of the woman.

The subsequent events, the plagues and Israel's escape from Egypt, become, for Old Testament believers, the ultimate expression of the Lord's saving work on their behalf. But it is saving work in the context of *judgement* on those who continue to oppose the Lord and his people. The Lord chooses to effect this saving work through an individual representative, Moses, to whom he declares: "I am the Lord and I will bring you out from under the burdens of the Egyptians, and I will deliver you from slavery to them, and I will redeem you with an outstretched arm and with great acts of judgement" (Exodus 6:6).

We might say that, in the providence of God, Joseph and his brothers were led to Egypt so that they might experience God's redeeming work: salvation by the grace of God. The Exodus is a huge signpost in the Old Testament story: an event frequently referred back to by psalmists and prophets alike. As such, it becomes a model or a preview (or a 'type', as Christian theologians would call it), of a greater Exodus, a greater work of redemption that God would one day bring about in and through the sacrificial, saving death of his Son, Jesus Christ, on the cross.

At the same time, we must not lose sight of the conflict element, and God's judging (cursing) those who oppose him and his people. Stephen G Dempster captures this well:

> "If Exodus is read in isolation from Genesis, then the Pharaoh is simply another obstacle, although a major

one, that the Israelites faced on their journey to nationhood. If, however, this text is viewed in the context of the geographical and genealogical dimensions of Genesis and in the wider context of that storyline as it unfolds, there is a more profound reason why blessing for the Israelites is a disaster for the Pharaoh. The series of events leading up to Hebrew genocide is seen to work out the struggle between the seed of the serpent and the seed of the woman..."[17]

Our big-picture, biblical theology reading of the Bible's storyline forces us to see that ultimately the promises of Genesis 12:1-3 are realised not in Abraham (or those who are merely his physical descendants), but in Jesus. He is the one through whom all kinds of people will be blessed. That means, of course, that the dishonouring referred to in Genesis 12:3 is also, ultimately, a dishonouring of Jesus, and the cursing will be the Lord's verdict on those who dishonour, or reject, Jesus. The world *will* dishonour and reject Jesus; it *hates* Jesus, as he himself declared. Those who remain, unrepentant, in this state of rebellion will one day face the curse of his judgement.

The many and the one

But it is important that we continue to see how this relates to the persecution of God's people. In the previous chapter we referred to the way the relationship between the corporate and the individual representative runs from Genesis 3:15 through the Bible's storyline. The promises of Genesis 12:3 reinforce this. To see that, it is helpful to return to the apostle Paul's application of this verse and of the overall place of Abraham in his letter to the Galatians.

Having referred to Genesis 12:3 as an anticipation of the

---

[17] Stephen G Dempter, *Dominion and Dynasty*, pp.93,94

gospel, Paul goes on to speak of Christ redeeming us from the *curse* of the law, "so that in Christ Jesus the blessing of Abraham might come to the Gentiles, so that we might receive the promised Spirit through faith" (Galatians 3:14). He then declares,

> "Now the promises were made to Abraham and to his offspring. It does not say, 'And to offsprings', referring to many, but referring to one, 'And to your offspring,' who is Christ." (Galatians 3:16)

The word offspring (seed) does not appear in Genesis 12:1-3, but it does crop up in subsequent promises to Abraham, from Genesis 15 onwards. Paul, it seems, deliberately latches on to the ambiguity created by the use of the singular word 'seed', to emphasise that the promises made to Abraham find their ultimate fulfilment in Christ and the gospel. And yet, at the end of the very same chapter, Paul writes,

> "... you are all one in Christ Jesus. And if you are Christ's, then you are Abraham's offspring, heirs according to promise." (Galatians 3:28b-29)

So the seed of Abraham is Jesus. The seed of Abraham is also those who are the followers of Jesus. Once again we see the tight relationship between the corporate and the individual representative. Once again we are reminded that the conflict between the seed of the woman and the seed of the serpent has an individual dimension and a corporate dimension.

In fact, Paul assumes this later in the letter. The teaching we have been referring to comes in the context of a serious pastoral situation: Paul writes to the Galatians because he is concerned that these Gentile Christians are being persuaded to add Jewish, Old Covenant elements (particularly the rite of circumcision) to the gospel. This, he urges them to see, would undermine the complete sufficiency of the cross of Christ. So Paul goes on to contrast two lines of people: those born of promise and those born of slavery (see Galatians 4:21-27). By now we might be getting used to referring to these as the seed of the woman and the seed of the serpent! Then Paul adds,

> "Now you, brothers, like Isaac, are children of promise. But just as at that time he who was born according to the flesh *persecuted* him who was born according to the Spirit, *so also it is now.*"
> (Galatians 4:28-29)

Isaac, as we have seen, inherited, as an individual, the promise of Genesis 12:3 from his father. Yet Ishmael's ill-treatment of Isaac (which is what Paul is referring to) becomes typical of the way that one group of people ("the world", to use Jesus' words) will treat the other group of people (those who belong to Jesus by faith).

Already, as we are tracing the theme of *promise* through Scripture, we are seeing two things. Firstly, that conflict seems to be, in some sense, what we might refer to as the flipside of promise; historically at least, it proves to be a case of 'two sides of the same coin'.

As God's promise begins to unfold, so conflict ensues as the world, the seed of the serpent, opposes God and his promises. Secondly, the trajectory in the story we are following leads us to an individual sufferer – Jesus – but also keeps suggesting that those who align themselves with him are caught up in the conflict – because they are also caught up in, and are recipients of, the promise.

OUR RESPONSE TO THE STORY SO FAR

"I will bless those who bless you, and him who dishonours you I will curse..." (Genesis 12:3). Whenever we read Genesis 12:1-3 our focus is, naturally (and rightly!), on the theme of blessing.

This is, after all, the dominant concept being sounded in these verses. But we should not ignore the double-sided statement in the first part of verse 3: in terms of where we are in the Bible's storyline, at that point we can say it appears that God's blessing *or cursing* of people will be related to the way they respond to Abraham.

But while we might detect partial, short-term fulfilments of this declaration within the life of Abraham and the Old Testament timeline, our big-picture, biblical theology reading of the Scriptures in their entirety has pointed us towards the ultimate fulfilment of God's words in Jesus Christ. So, in terms of the complete storyline of the Bible, God's blessing or cursing of people will be related to the way they respond to *Jesus*. God will bless those who bless Jesus and will curse those who dishonour him. That's how we should read what is being said in Genesis 12:1-3 today, for such a reading respects the God-given trajectory in the Bible's storyline.

Dishonouring Jesus

How does the world dishonour Jesus? In any and every way in which it refuses to recognise him for who he truly is, and for what he has truly done for us. The world dishonours Jesus when it refuses to trust in him alone for the mercy and forgiveness it needs from the one true God. It dishonours him when it fails to worship and serve him as the rightful Lord of all.

And it also dishonours Jesus when it persecutes his followers.

We began this book with Jesus' words at the Last Supper, warning his disciples of persecution (John 15:18-21). In one sense, our tracing of the twin themes of promise and conflict through the storyline of the Bible is an exercise in bringing us to a greater, clearer understanding of why Jesus said what he said that night – and the ongoing relevance of those words for us today. "All these things they will do to you *on account of my name*," said Jesus (John 15:21).

How did the world express its hatred – its dishonour – of

Jesus when he was incarnate on the earth? By opposing him and finally by crucifying him.

How does the world express its hatred - its dishonour - of Jesus today? One significant way it does that is by the way it treats his followers. In the West, where Christianity has sunk deep cultural roots over many years, that dishonouring of Christ may have been characterised largely by a tendency to ignore him - or perhaps, at worst, to mock him and ridicule those who follow him. In many parts of the world, we know it is a different story: the hatred of Christ, the dishonouring of Christ, is expressed in the violent, oppressive persecution of his people. Even in the West, where freedom of religion has long been an accepted way of life, we have, in recent years, seen a growing intolerance of and hostility towards those who uphold and proclaim a true, biblical Christianity.

So, having reached the twelfth chapter of the Bible, we can already say that God is promising an individual seed of the woman who will conquer evil. This promise will be realised through a descendant of Abraham, and will mean God's blessing on those who embrace this descendant. All who reject God's saving plan - by dishonouring this individual - will be under God's curse.

The persecution of Christians is one of the most vivid ways in which that rejection of God's promise is demonstrated. But how should Christians respond?

Loving the haters

In the great promise made to Abraham, God makes it clear that it is *he* who will curse those who dishonour his chosen one. At this stage in the story we don't know when that will be fully and finally realised. So what are God's people to do in the meantime? At the end of the book of Deuteronomy, as God's people are encamped ready to enter the Promised Land, the Lord says through Moses:

> "Vengeance is mine, and recompense,
>   for the time when their foot shall slip;
> for the day of their calamity is at hand,
>   and their doom comes swiftly."
>   (Deuteronomy 32:35)

The apostle Paul quotes this verse at a significant moment in his letter to the Romans. In the twelfth chapter of that letter, Paul begins to spell out the implications, in this life, of the gospel he has so magnificently explained in the preceding chapters. This twelfth chapter of Romans focuses on our relationships, both within the body of Christ and with the world. Regarding the latter Paul writes:

> "Bless those who persecute you; *bless* and do not *curse* them... Beloved, never avenge yourselves, but leave it to the wrath of God, for it is written, 'Vengeance is mine, I will repay, says the Lord.' To the contrary, 'if your enemy is hungry, feed him; if he is thirsty, give him something to drink; for by so doing you will heap burning coals on his head.' Do not be overcome by evil, but overcome evil with good."
>   (Romans 12:14, 19-21)

Paul's words at the beginning of that paragraph echo the teaching of Jesus. In the Sermon on the Mount in Matthew's Gospel, we hear Jesus say: "... I say to you, love your enemies and pray for those who persecute you..." (Matthew 5:44). A parallel account in Luke's Gospel complements this: "... Love your enemies, do good to those who hate you, bless those who curse you, pray for those who abuse you" (Luke 6:27-28). In the Bible God blesses us (as we have seen in this chapter), we bless God (in the sense of ascribing to him the praise that is his due) and we also bless others (which implies invoking, or at least desiring and praying for, God's blessing on them).

The second Old Testament quotation in Paul's exhortation (Romans 12:20) comes from Proverbs 25:21-22. Taken as a whole, the paragraph serves to remind us that it is not sufficient merely to refrain from retaliatory actions – while perhaps, deep down, gleefully comforting ourselves with the thought that one day our persecutors will suffer the incomprehensibly awe-inspiring wrath of God! No, we are to bless: we are to do them good. It is in that context that we should understand the reference to heaping burning coals on their heads. While a few commentators down the years have understood "burning coals" to be a reference to future divine punishment, most recognise that this does not fit the context. What is in view is the effect that our ministering to our enemies' needs has on them *now*. Our loving actions may shame them and induce remorse; they may even – by the grace of God (and when accompanied by the preaching of the gospel) – lead our persecutors to true repentance, and to a saving knowledge of the Lord Jesus.

Precisely because God will finally curse – that is, judge – those who dishonour Jesus Christ, we his people are to go on holding out the gospel in love to those who dishonour Jesus today. That must include those who persecute his followers.

A biblical response to a biblical understanding of persecution will include a desire to respond to hatred with love; a desire to go on offering Christ to those who, in the very act of persecuting Christians, are expressing a rejection of Christ.

2 Samuel 7:8-13

"...Thus says the Lord of hosts, I took you from the pasture, from following the sheep, that you should be prince over my people Israel. And I have been with you wherever you went and have cut off all your enemies from before you. And I will make for you a great name, like the name of the great ones of the earth. And I will appoint a place for my people Israel and will plant them, so that they may dwell in their own place and be disturbed no more. And violent men shall afflict them no more, as formerly, from the time that I appointed judges over my people Israel. And I will give you rest from all your enemies. Moreover, the Lord declares to you that the Lord will make you a house. When your days are fulfilled and you lie down with your fathers, I will raise up your offspring after you, who shall come from your body, and I will establish his kingdom. He shall build a house for my name, and I will establish the throne of his kingdom forever."

5. The Promise *completed*

EVERY good storyline has its twists and turns, moments when something in the plot catches us by surprise. The Bible springs one such surprise on us in its storyline at the end of the book of Genesis.

What have we discovered so far about God's promise? In the face of mankind's rebellion (and the declared consequences of such rebellion), God offers enigmatic words of hope, even as he speaks a word of judgement to the tempting serpent (Genesis 3:15). Mankind will not be extinguished: God's words imply the story will continue! Moreover, God's words of judgement imply that a descendant ('seed') of the woman will defeat the serpent.

As we move through generations of descendants, the human race appears to keep dividing into two: those who belong to God and the godless. God acts in judgement – but also acts in grace, to perpetuate the line through which he will fulfil his promise.

This first part of the story arrives at a significant moment with God's call of Abraham. To the initial promise-in-judgement of victory in Genesis 3:15, God adds the promise of blessing. The words to the serpent had spoken of an individual ("*He* shall bruise your head"); now it is to Abraham, as an individual, that God says, "In you all the families of the earth shall be blessed."

We have observed how these promises, when traced along the trajectory of Scripture, speak of Jesus and the gospel. He is the seed of the woman who will conquer. He is the descendant of Abraham who will bless.

We have also discovered that conflict is present in the midst of God's promises. From the way the story begins it seems that this conflict is engendered in the godless as they react to those promises of God. This, too, can be traced to Jesus and the gospel, as the world expresses its hatred of Jesus and, in doing so, demonstrates its ignorance of God himself. This conflict impacts not just on the chosen individual, however, but also on all who are aligned with him.

Put in those terms, we might say that already we have seen enough of God's story to appreciate what a fundamental factor the persecution of God's people is within that story, and why persecution is inevitable. Persecution will be present as long as the world continues to be hostile to the gospel. But we need to follow the story to the end, both for our encouragement and so we are better equipped to respond, prayerfully and pastorally, as God would have us do.

Jacob and his sons

Genesis chapters 12-50 focus on just four generations of one family. God's promises of blessing to Abraham are, as we noted earlier, passed on first to Isaac and then to Jacob.

In Genesis 49, Jacob blesses his sons or, more accurately, tells them "what shall happen to you in days to come" (Genesis 49:1). In the context of reading the bigger story, we ought to be alert to see the direction in which *God's* (ultimate) promise of blessing is going. One possible candidate, we might think, could be Reuben, on the grounds that he is the firstborn (although the choice of Jacob over Esau – see Genesis 25:23-26 – has already suggested that God does not necessarily stick to that principle!)

A second, arguably stronger candidate might be Joseph, for several reasons. First, his story has dominated since chapter 37, and he has been set above his brothers who, in their jealousy and hatred, conspire to get rid of him. Despite the suffering his brothers have caused him, Joseph is clearly *blessed* by the Lord, at least in the short term (eg Genesis 39:3, 23). Second, Joseph is evidently a saviour-type figure: he himself acknowledges how God, in his sovereignty, has used Joseph's suffering to bring about the saving of his people (see Genesis 45:5; 50:20). Finally, when Jacob accepts Joseph's two sons, Manasseh and Ephraim, as his own (Genesis 48:5), he declares that nations will spring from Ephraim (Genesis 48:19). It looks like Joseph's line, then, will take up the mantle. However, a surprise is in store…

THE PROMISE OF A KING!

Jacob's sons hear mixed messages from their father as to their futures. Joseph *does* hear some significant words of blessing (Genesis 49:22-26) but surprisingly it is to Judah, Jacob's fourth-born, that attention now turns.

> "Judah, your brothers shall praise you;
>   your hand shall be on the neck of your enemies;
>   your father's sons shall bow down before you.
> Judah is a lion's cub;
>   From the prey, my son, you have gone up.
> He stooped down; he crouched as a lion
>   and as a lioness; who dares rouse him?
> The sceptre shall not depart from Judah,
>   nor the ruler's staff from between his feet,
> until tribute comes to him;
>   and to him shall be the obedience of the
>   peoples." (Genesis 49:8-10)

That final verse uses clear royal terminology. A *king* is going to come from the line of Judah! The verse is hinting at the next significant stage of the storyline. This royal language crops up again in the rather strange account of the false prophet, Balaam. In the book of Numbers we read of Israel's journey towards the Promised Land. The Moabite king Balak, fearful of this advance, employs Balaam to curse the Israelites. Balaam is, in many ways, a curious character. Although corrupt and willing to be employed to curse God's people, his intentions are repeatedly overruled by the sovereign hand of the Lord, who speaks words of *blessing* through him. Balaam ends his third oracle declaring of Israel:

> "He crouched, he lay down like a lion
> and like a lioness; who will rouse him up?
> Blessed are those who bless you,
>   and cursed are those who curse you."
>   (Numbers 24:9)

How would Moses' audience at the time have understood this? And what should we therefore notice about these words? They seem deliberate in combining imagery from Jacob's words about Judah in Genesis 49:9 with God's blessing of Abraham in Genesis 12:3. It seems that the promise made to Abraham - that all kinds of people would ultimately be blessed in and through him - will be fulfilled through this coming king from Judah! Then in his final oracle Balaam says,

> "I see him, but not now;
>   I behold him, but not near:
> a star shall come out of Jacob,
>   and a sceptre shall rise out of Israel;
> it shall crush the forehead of Moab..."
>   (Numbers 24:17)

Once again the language of a coming king is employed. Some would argue that a reference to crushing the forehead of Moab is also an allusion to the original promise of Genesis 3:15 - that a seed of the woman will bruise the head of the serpent! The promises are continuing to develop. Balaam's enforced blessing of them should have served to encourage God's pilgrim people. James Hamilton sums up well how the threads can be drawn together at this point in the story:

> "God would fulfil the promises to Abraham through

the King from Judah, who is the seed of the woman who would crush the head of the serpent and his seed, and in this way God would accomplish the purposes he began at creation."[18]

Moses speaks further of the coming king in Deuteronomy 17:14-20, warning the people not to choose a king according to the standards of the world. However, in Samuel's day that warning is not heeded, and Saul is eventually chosen as the first king. His failure leads the Lord to choose David, the son of Jesse, "a man after his own heart" (1 Samuel 13:14). David is, for some time, pursued (that is, persecuted) by Saul, but the Lord protects him until finally he is anointed as king, which brings us to the verses that introduced this chapter. 2 Samuel 7 - the covenant with David - is another huge signpost in the Old Testament storyline.

The covenant with David

The context is David's expressed desire to build a house for the Lord and for the Ark of the Covenant. The Lord's response comes through the prophet Nathan and contains a play on words. David had contemplated building a 'house' (a building) for the Lord, but the Lord will in fact build a 'house' (a dynasty) for David (2 Samuel 7:11).

God's covenant promise to David is made at a time, we are told, when "the Lord had given him rest from all his surrounding enemies" (2 Samuel 7:1). And yet, at the same time, among the various key promises of this chapter, the Lord declares to David: "And I *will* give you rest from all your enemies" (2 Samuel 7:11). Evidently there is more still to come in this story.

Mention of "rest" here sounds like the absence of conflict; the conflict, we have already noted, that manifests itself in the

---

[18] Hamilton, *What is Biblical Theology?*, pp.47,48

hostility towards, and persecution of, God's people by their enemies, by those who are not followers of the Lord. So when will this promise be fulfilled? When will this rest be fully and finally established and experienced? When will God's people no longer face the threat of persecution by their enemies? Not in the time of David, evidently. Although, in subsequent chapters, he enjoys victories over the Philistines (2 Samuel 8), the Ammonites and the Syrians (2 Samuel 10), he nevertheless faces the lengthy conflict engendered by his own son, Absalom, as well as further rebellion led by the Benjaminite Sheba (2 Samuel 14-21).

The climax to God's covenant declaration comes with the reference to David's son:

> "When your days are fulfilled and you lie down with your fathers, I will raise up your offspring after you, who shall come from your body, and I will establish his kingdom. He shall build a house for my name, and I will establish the throne of his kingdom forever. I will be to him a father, and he shall be to me a son..." (2 Samuel 7:12-14)

Solomon and beyond

As the story unfolds, it appears that this is referring to Solomon who does, indeed, build a house (building) for the Lord in Jerusalem.

In one sense, the Old Testament storyline then reaches what appears to be a natural resolution or climax in 1 Kings 8. Solomon builds the temple and we are told:

> "And when the priests came out of the Holy Place, a cloud filled the house of the Lord, so that the priests could not stand to minister because of the cloud, for the *glory of the Lord* filled the house of the Lord." (1 Kings 8:10-11)

This is reminiscent of what happened when Moses completed the Tabernacle (see Exodus 40:34-35). The Tabernacle and its successor, the Temple, were identified by the Lord as the place of the Lord's presence or dwelling; the place where the Lord met with his people; the place, consequently, where sin was atoned for. As Solomon dedicates the Temple and blesses the people, he declares,

> "Blessed be the Lord who has given rest to his people Israel, according to all that he promised. Not one word has failed of all his good promise, which he spoke by Moses his servant." (1 Kings 8:56)

So that's it, then? All the promises fulfilled? The story is at an end, it seems. And they all lived happily ever after. Roll the credits. Cue the closing theme music. Except – no: that's not where the story ends. In fact, as we read on from 1 Kings 8, things start to go wrong very quickly. Sadly, we are told, Solomon turns to other gods in his old age (1 Kings 11:4) and, in the generation that follows him, in-fighting leads to the kingdom being divided. What follows is a generally dismal account of failed individuals reigning – particularly in the north. The northern kingdom (now referred to as Israel) is eventually swallowed up by the Assyrian empire (see 2 Kings 17:6). Despite the intervention of prophets and the occasional attempt at reform by a faithful king, the southern kingdom (Judah) then subsequently falls to the Babylonians (see 2 Kings 24-25). It is made clear that this disastrous sequence of events comes about because of the idolatrous rebellion of the people. In many ways, the largely sorry saga of 1 and 2 Kings can be summed up, theologically, by the extended comment in 2 Kings 17:7-23. Notice how the southern kingdom is included in the condemnation (verse 19).

One way or another, at this point in the storyline, we have yet to see the final rest that was promised to David. We have yet to see the final victory of the seed of the woman. That means, inevitably, we have yet to see an end to opposition and hostility experienced by the people of God. If God's promises are going to come to fruition, there must be more still to come.

THE CONFLICT – "HOW LONG, O LORD?"

This chapter is titled 'The Promise completed', which might raise a few eyebrows. After all, David lived and reigned about a thousand years before the birth of Jesus. A lot of water (much of it murky) passes under the proverbial bridge between those two points in the Bible's storyline. In what sense, then, can we say that the covenant with David completes God's promises?

Abraham to David to Christ

We have just noted that the storyline reaches what appears to be a climax with the building of Solomon's Temple. If we were to take another peek at later parts of the storyline we would observe that one striking feature of the New Testament's presentation of the gospel is the way it references, or summarises, the Old Testament story. Time and again, writers and preachers seem to take us from Abraham to David (sometimes via Moses and the Exodus) – and then make a jump to Christ. We observe this in Matthew's genealogy (with the additional reference to the exile). Peter's Pentecost Day sermon (Acts 2) moves from David to Christ. Paul's sermon in Pisidian Antioch (Acts 13) does the same. Stephen adds a reference to Solomon carrying out David's intention to build a Temple, before making the same historic leap (Acts 7). Is this coincidence?

No, it isn't. In terms of the historical storyline there is an obvious progression from Abraham to David (if we include, under David, the beginning of Solomon's reign, up to the building of the Temple), as God's people enter the Promised Land and eventually appear to receive all of God's promises. But then decline sets in, and opposition from those opposed to the promises of God continues (and even increases). What are God's people to make of all this? Moreover, how are hope and promise maintained in the near thousand-year interval? The answer is through the medium of the prophets.

The era of the prophets

In the light of the failure that followed the time of Solomon, the prophets frequently look *back* to the whole Abraham-to-David story and use language, events and symbols from that past era – particularly from the time of the Exodus – in order to look *forward* to a greater work that God will one day do, to fulfil his promises fully and finally. It is within this context that we hear the promise of a new covenant, couched in terms of God's law (Jeremiah 31:31-34) and of David (Ezekiel 37:24-28). The hope of a greater David, an ideal David, grows. This we know as the Messianic hope.

This prophetic hope embraces concepts of salvation, reconciliation and restoration to God – but also the final victory over those who are enemies of God and his people.

Many of these themes are prominent, for example, in the majestic book of the prophet Isaiah – a book which says much about God's judgement, but which also holds out much in the way of hope. In chapter 11, Isaiah clearly has the promises of 2 Samuel 7 to David in mind when he speaks of a future "shoot from the stump of Jesse" (Isaiah 11:1). This figure will bring about what can only be described as a return to the conditions of Eden (Isaiah 11:6-7). Isaiah's reference to the nursing child playing over the hole of the cobra and the weaned child putting his hand on the adder's den (Isaiah 11:8) may be another allusion to the original victory promise of Genesis 3:15. At the same time, this promised individual "shall strike the earth with the rod of his mouth, and with the breath of his lips he shall kill the wicked" (Isaiah 11:4). This future David will have the victory.

In a section often referred to as his Little Apocalypse (chapters 24-27), Isaiah combines images that speak of the *blessing* of restoration and atonement (Isaiah 27:9), victory over a serpent (Isaiah 27:1), judgement on a rebellious world (Isaiah 24:6-8) and an end to the opposition and hostility being experienced by his people ("...and the Lord God will wipe away tears from all faces, and the *reproach* of his people he will take away from all the earth..." (Isaiah 25:8).

What is the response to this?

> "It will be said on that day,
>   'Behold, this is our God; we have waited for him,
>   that he might save us.
>   This is the Lord; we have waited for him;
>   let us be glad and rejoice in his salvation."
>
>   (Isaiah 25:9)

But this final victory – a victory that should elicit rejoicing – was not experienced in Isaiah's day. In fact, the prophet lived during that most troubled of times, amid national crises that would culminate in the exile to Babylon (see references to Isaiah in 2 Kings 19-20).

God's promise – then and now – is intended to produce in his people the dual response of faith and hope. God's faithful people in Isaiah's day (however few in number!) were to trust God's promises *despite* their present circumstances. Those present circumstances would include the ongoing hostility of those who are opposed to God. The same is true for us today.

In a real sense this perspective prevails right through to the end of the Old Testament. Although, in time, God's people return from exile, the conditions they find themselves in afterwards clearly fall short of the ideal envisaged by the prophets. Jerusalem's walls are repaired and a new Temple built, but this Temple does not even seem to match Solomon's, in terms of splendour. Yes, if God is going to keep his promises, more is still to come.

OUR RESPONSE TO THE STORY SO FAR

In this chapter we have seen how God's progressive, developing promises have reached an apparent crescendo in the time of David and his son, Solomon. God is going to defeat evil and the serpent through a seed of the woman, who will be a descendant of Abraham, who will come from the tribe of Judah, and who will be a royal son of David.

And yet events that followed the time of Solomon's Temple building seem to call into question the worth of God's promises.

We have also noted how the prophets then treat that whole storyline up to the time of David – namely, as an anticipation, a preview, a type of a yet-to-come greater work of salvation.

How does this part of the storyline help us today when we wrestle with the reality of the persecution of Christians around the world?

We saw that the prophets' message was intended to maintain and strengthen *faith* and *hope*. Biblical faith is, in essence, belief and trust in the promises of God, and in those promises we find our hope, even in the midst of persecution. Perseverance in faith and hope – in the face of opposition from the world – is also a dominant theme in the book of Psalms.

Faith and hope in the Psalms

Down the centuries, the Psalms have continued to be one of the most treasured parts of the Bible for many Christians, expressing as they do faith in God in all the circumstances of life. In recent times, though, there has been something of a recovery of the value of seeing the Psalms as a book, with something of a coherent progression and message, rather than simply a random collection of 150 quite independent prayers or hymns.[19]

---

[19] I say 'recovery' as, at different times in church history, there have been people who have emphasised reading the Psalms as a 'whole'. For example, Martin Luther, the German Protestant Reformer, referred to the Psalms as "a little Bible". Further back in history, Basil, the Bishop of Caesarea, referred to the Psalms as "a compendium of all theology".

It would be straying from our theme to go into this in any great depth,[20] but even a cursory reflection on the Psalms suggests, I believe, an overall purpose or structure.

First, the Psalms are divided up into five books (Psalms 1-41; 42-72; 73-89; 90-106; 107-150) and the books finish with similar, single-verse endings that at times seem out of place with the content of the individual Psalm they conclude (see and compare Psalm 41:13; 72:19; 89:52; 106:48. It is sometimes then argued that the whole of Psalms 146-150 provides a grand 'Hallelujah' ending to the collection as a whole).

Second, there seems to be a *general* movement from lament to praise as we progress through the collection. In other words, there is evidence, within the Psalms themselves, of a deliberate ordering. This ordering may well have taken place after the return from exile, as the existing Psalms were compiled into the structure we now have, with the deliberate intention of mirroring the experience of God's people.

So the hostility and persecution David faced early in his life is evident in Psalms 3-41. David's reign appears to give way to Solomon's at the end of Book 2 (Psalm 72). Book 3 seems to mirror the decline recorded in 1 & 2 Kings, and ends (Psalm 89) with a reflection on the painful contrast between God's promises and faithfulness in the past (Psalm 89:1-37) and the present disaster of exile (Psalm 89:38-51). The short Book 4 sounds the repeated message that "the Lord reigns!" (that is, he is *still* king – despite what has happened) and ends with a plea that God would gather his people from exile (Psalm 106:47). Book 5 then looks to future restoration (as the prophets did), embracing more Psalms of David (as the prophets used David) to restate and reaffirm hope.

Such an approach helps us to see that the Psalms are not simply individual, disconnected poems that offer an outlet for

---

[20] For those who wish to do so, I would recommend O Palmer Robertson, *The Flow of the Psalms* (Phillipsburg, P&R Publishing, 2015), or James M Hamilton Jr, *God's Glory in Salvation through Judgement* (Wheaton: Crossway, 2010), pp.275-290.

personal expressions of emotion; they are inextricably bound up with the Bible's storyline – and that means they are bound up with God's promises. Reading (praying) the Psalms sequentially (as has often been the practice of believers in the past) can help reinforce for us the direction of the Bible's story (a story that is leading to Jesus), and so strengthen and sustain that faith and hope – even in the midst of the world's hatred and hostility.

Take Psalm 72, for example. It has the superscription "Of Solomon". This could mean either that it was written *by* Solomon, or that it was written *for* Solomon, perhaps by David. Either way, the final verse ("The prayers of David, the son of Jesse, are ended") suggests we have reached that historical climax we referred to earlier, at the crossover between the end of David's reign and Solomon's building of the Temple.

Psalm 72 itself presents the son of David, the king, in the grandest of terms and in an idealistic way that goes far beyond anything the historical David (or those who followed him) could ever amount to. In doing so, it also seems to gather up the promises we have been tracking along the storyline so far. References to "crushing the oppressor" (verse 4) and enemies "licking the dust" (verse 9) remind us of the first promise-in-judgement of Genesis 3:15, while verse 17 declares:

> "May his name endure forever,
>   his fame continue as long as the sun!
> May people be blessed in him,
>   all nations call him blessed!" (Psalm 72:17)

This clearly links the Davidic king – who is the subject of the Psalm – with the promise of blessing made to Abraham in Genesis 12:1-3. There is, indeed, both unity and progression in the story of God's promise!

Incidentally, Christians sometimes puzzle over that final verse of Psalm 72, given the fact that there *are* more Psalms attributed to David later in the collection. But if the Psalms were ordered deliberately to mirror the experience of God's people thus far, it does make sense to indicate where in the story we should place Psalm 72. Additional Psalms of David used later in the collection reflect the hope for the future: that the ideal David, the David of the prophets, will one day appear to fulfil all of God's promises, fully and finally.

Much more could be said, but before we close this chapter we ought to note the significance for our overall subject of Psalms 1 and 2.

Psalms 1 and 2

Taken together, these two Psalms constitute a double introduction to the whole collection of Psalms and sum up its major themes. Several observations suggest the two Psalms should be considered together. They open and close with the theme of blessing (Psalm 1:1; 2:12b), and they both close with the threat of perishing (Psalm 1:6; 2:12a). Also, they both combine that interplay between the individual and corporate that we considered in Chapter 3 (e.g. the blessed "man" of Psalm 1:1-3 and the "congregation" of the righteous in Psalm 1:5-6; the "Anointed" one of Psalm 2:2 and all the "blessed" who take refuge in him in Psalm 2:12).

Psalm 1 refers to two different (even mutually exclusive) types of people, the blessed/righteous man and the wicked. By now we might almost instinctively think of them as the seed of the woman and the seed of the serpent.

What characterises the blessed man is a love for God's word, or law (Psalm 1:1-2). This is followed by a wonderful description of his fruitfulness (Psalm 1:3). The prophet Jeremiah would later pick up on this imagery, adding to it the comment that the blessed man "trusts in the Lord" (Jeremiah 17:7-8). It is those who first trust in the Lord, and who therefore belong to the Lord, who love his word and seek to follow it, rather than following the "counsel of the wicked". At the same time, the emphasis on the singular person at the beginning of the Psalm

("Blessed is the man...", "He is like a tree...") reminds us that, ultimately, this Psalm points us to Jesus. Only he has perfectly delighted in and obeyed God's word. He is that individual seed of the woman. But the "congregation of the righteous" are those who are united to him; they are the corporate seed of the woman; they are those who are "known" by the Lord (Psalm 1:6).

The wicked, we are told, are "like chaff that the wind drives away" (Psalm 1:4) and they "will not stand in the judgement" (Psalm 1:5). They and their ways will "perish" (Psalm 1:6). The wicked – and, crucially, all that they do – will not endure. Their time will pass. What an encouragement that is for those facing the reality of persecution!

If the emphasis in Psalm 1 is on the ways of the blessed man, this shifts in Psalm 2 to those who "take counsel together, against the Lord and *against his Anointed...*" (Psalm 2:2). In contrast to the blessed man who delights in God's word, these rebels consider God's ways to be like repressive chains that they need to break free from (Psalm 2:3). The Lord's response is to declare that he has appointed his Anointed one as the king (Psalm 2:4-6), who will one day rule over all the nations (Psalm 2:7-9). In the light of the certainty of that declaration, the final three verses (Psalm 2:10-12) then read like an evangelistic appeal to come to the Lord and his anointed.

Psalm 2 is a favourite among New Testament writers, and it is particularly interesting for us here to see how it is used in Acts 4. The apostles have just had their first taste of the persecution that followed Christ's ascension, when Peter and John were arrested for preaching in Jesus the eschatological resurrection from the dead (Acts 4:2). After being held in custody overnight they are warned, before being released, not to speak further in the name of Jesus (Acts 4:1-22). When the two rejoin their friends, they all pray. As they reflect on their experience, they recall Psalm 2. But what is noteworthy is that, although it is the suffering of *Peter and John* that has occasioned this impromptu prayer meeting, the disciples declare that the actions of the ungodly alliance in Psalm 2 have found their fulfilment in the suffering of *Jesus* (Acts 4:23-28).

In other words, they instinctively recognise that their own suffering can, and should, be traced back to the world's hostility towards their Lord. This is, of course, precisely what Jesus had told them at the Last Supper. Whenever Christians are persecuted, for being Christians, for preaching the gospel, for simply acknowledging that Jesus Christ is Lord, it is important, pastorally, to be able to link their experience with the biblical testimony to the way the world rails against Christ himself.

It is also important to see the long-term perspective of Psalms 1 and 2. Because they serve to introduce major themes that will unfold in the rest of the Psalms, and because the book of Psalms as a whole moves in the direction of hope for the future, we need to see how these two Psalms should sustain that hope in us.

That wonderful picture of the fruitfulness of the righteous one, for example (Psalm 1:3-4) does not support a prosperity gospel message for the here and now, any more than description of the wicked as chaff means their wickedness will come to an end any time soon. One only has to read David's prayers through the rest of Book 1 (Psalms 3-41) to see that hostility from those who are opposed to God continues. Rather, Psalm 1 lifts our eyes above and beyond our present circumstances to what will be revealed in the judgement that is to come (Psalm 1:5).

In other words, Psalms 1 and 2 offer us what we would refer to as an *eschatological* perspective: they set before us the long-term certainties of God's promise and God's unfolding plan – because these are the things that will sustain our faith and hope, even in the midst of present suffering. We saw earlier that the new covenant promise is couched in terms of God's law (Jeremiah 31:31-34) and of a future David (Ezekiel 37:24-28); Psalms 1 and 2, in their description of the blessed one and the anointed king, echo this.

We also noted earlier that there is a general movement through the book of Psalms from lament to praise. This in itself is an important reason for seeing the book of Psalms as a book with a coherent structure. The Psalms of lament remind us it *is* appropriate to cry out to God in the midst of suffering, and to acknowledge the perplexities that this suffering creates. We cannot fully understand why God allows his people to suffer persecution for their faith in him and for proclaiming Christ to others. But lament does not mean, in faith terms, utter despair. The psalmists' cries are cries to the God they still believe in and trust.

At the same time, true biblical faith is forward-looking. Our hope, ultimately, is not for this life, but for the promised Messianic kingdom. The flow of the Psalms (coupled with the message of the prophetic books) helps us see the tension between what is now and what one day will be. By God's grace, as we learn to focus on the latter, this will sustain in us, and in all God's suffering people, a true faith and a sure hope.

Matthew 2:13-18

"Now when they had departed, behold, an angel of the Lord appeared to Joseph in a dream and said, 'Rise, take the child and his mother, and flee to Egypt, and remain there until I tell you, for Herod is about to search for the child, to destroy him.' And he rose and took the child and his mother by night and departed to Egypt and remained there until the death of Herod. This was to fulfil what the Lord had spoken by the prophet, 'Out of Egypt I called my son.'

Then Herod, when he saw that he had been tricked by the wise men, became furious, and he sent and killed all the male children in Bethlehem and in all that region who were two years old or under, according to the time that he had ascertained from the wise men. Then was fulfilled what was spoken by the prophet Jeremiah:

'A voice was heard in Ramah,
    Weeping and loud lamentation,
Rachel weeping for her children;
    she refused to be comforted, because
        they are no more.'"

6. The Promise *fulfilled*

IN the providence of God it is the Gospel of Matthew that launches us into the New Testament section of our Bibles.

Matthew sets out to write the most amazing, captivating and certainly significant life story of all time... and he begins with a genealogy! Yes, another of those lists... But what a genealogy this is! And what a beginning: "The book of the genealogy of Jesus Christ, the son of David, the son of Abraham" (Matthew 1:1).

If you have been following the story so far, that verse should arrive with the force of an express train!

The kingly descendant

In one sense, there may have been many people in Matthew's day who could trace their lineage back through David and the tribe of Judah to Abraham – but Matthew means us to see something special here. He declares that this Jesus of whom he is about to write is the Christ, or Messiah; the anointed one: that is, the one spoken of by the prophets.

In other words, Matthew announces up-front the bold claim that the person he is going to write about is the one who truly fulfils all of God's promises. He is *the* son of David, whose throne, according to 2 Samuel 7, God would establish forever. He is *the* descendent of Abraham who, according to Genesis 12:1-3, would be the means by which all kinds of people will receive eternal blessing from God. Although Matthew doesn't mention the original promise-in-judgement of Genesis 3:15, we have already seen how, in earlier parts of the storyline, the connections are made between this and later expressions of

God's promises. That means Jesus is also *the* individual seed of the woman who will conquer the serpent and his seed.

From the outset, then, Matthew is preparing us to read the story of Jesus in terms of promise and fulfilment. This story of Jesus does not exist in a vacuum. It is part of the storyline of God; indeed, it is the climax of that storyline. Phrases such as "This was to fulfil what the Lord had spoken..." crop up frequently in Matthew, especially in the opening chapters. However, as we begin to read Matthew's account, we naturally want to know precisely *how* those promises will be fulfilled in Jesus. The answer initially surprised many of his followers, and helps us understand more about the fundamental nature of persecution in this present age.

PROMISE FULFILLED IN JESUS

Matthew's genealogy of Jesus is followed by his account of the virgin birth (Matthew 1:18-25). This is declared to be in fulfilment of God's word (Matthew 1:22-23, quoting Isaiah 7:14) and names Jesus as Immanuel, 'God with us'. We said earlier that the Old Testament storyline leaves us with the feeling that more is still to come. In the coming of Jesus, God fulfils his promises in a more amazing way than even those original, individual promises might suggest. He fulfils them in the incarnation of his eternal son!

In chapter 2 Matthew then recounts the well-known story of the visit by the wise men (magi), who follow a star to Bethlehem, and who acknowledge Jesus as king, and express worship by giving Mary and Joseph some incredibly luxurious gifts.

The promise to Abraham was that through him "all the families of the earth shall be blessed" (Genesis 12:3). The visit of the wise men is suggestive, at least, of this promise beginning to be fulfilled. We don't know too much about them, other than that they were "from the east" (Matthew 2:1). Babylon is often considered their likely place of origin. Almost certainly they were Gentiles, and yet here they are, seeking and worshipping the one they believed to be the Messiah.

We might add here that Matthew's Gospel ends on the same note with which it begins. In the so-called Great Commission, the risen Lord Jesus declares to his followers: "All authority in heaven and on earth has been given to me. Go therefore and make disciples *of all nations*..." (Matthew 28:18-19). Jesus is the true descendent of Abraham, through whom all kinds of people will be blessed.

As the episode recorded in Matthew 2 unfolds, the attitude and response of these wise men is contrasted with that of the Jewish priests in Jerusalem and especially King Herod. We will come back to Herod in the 'Victory in conflict' shortly, but, before we do, it is valuable to note further signals Matthew gives us of how Jesus is fulfilling the promises of God (particularly in the verses quoted at the beginning of this chapter).

God takes unusual, specific action at several points in the story, speaking through dreams to preserve and protect his anointed one. As a result of one such dream, Joseph takes Mary and their baby to Egypt, to escape the murderous intent of Herod. Matthew tells us: "This was to fulfil what the Lord had spoken by the prophet, 'Out of Egypt I called my son'" (Matthew 2:15). The quotation is from Hosea 11:1. In its original setting, the prophet Hosea is referring to the *people of Israel* coming out of Egypt at the Exodus. What is Matthew doing with scripture?

He is doing biblical theology! He is tracing a theme through the trajectory of scripture, to find its proper fulfilment in Christ and the gospel.

Jesus as the true Israel

Hosea 11 contains a warning for the short term, but hope for the longer term. The prophet reminds the people that, although God redeemed them from Egypt at the Exodus, and then continued to care for them, they have nonetheless continued to rebel against him (Hosea 11:1-4). As a result, they will suffer at the hands of their enemies (Hosea 11:5). We know this eventually meant exile. And yet, in the latter part of the chapter, God reaffirms his steadfast love for his people. In this they are to hope.

But although Hosea 11 is referring to the people of Israel as a whole, the chapter begins, as we have seen, by referring to them as an individual: "When Israel was a child, I loved *him*, and out of Egypt I called my son" (Hosea 11:1). Israel had been referred to in this way at the time of the Exodus itself:

> "Then you shall say to Pharaoh, 'Thus says the Lord, Israel is my firstborn son, and I say to you, "Let my son go that he may serve me." If you refuse to let him go, behold, I will kill your firstborn son.'"
> (Exodus 4:22-23)

Without the quotation from Hosea 11:1, Matthew's account (in Matthew 2:13-15) would still read as a powerful declaration of God's providential care of his Messiah. So what does the quotation add – and why does Matthew add it? It suggests something very important about Jesus. In declaring that Hosea 11:1 is fulfilled in the life of Jesus, Matthew is saying that Jesus is the embodiment of Israel. He is the true Israel. All that Israel was meant to be will be found to be true in him.

This takes us back to the observation we made when considering Genesis 3:15, namely: the creative tension that exists in God's word between the many and the one, between the collective group and an individual who stands as representative. This concept is so important for a proper understanding of sin, of salvation, of our status before God in Christ – and also of the spiritual significance of the persecution of Christians by a world living in rebellion against God and actively rejecting his Son.

As far as sin and salvation are concerned, the apostle Paul reminds us: "For as in Adam all die, so also in Christ shall all be made alive" (1 Corinthians 15:22). As far as our status before God in Christ is concerned, Paul writes: "For our sake [God] made [Christ] to be sin who knew no sin, so that in him we might become the righteousness of God" (2 Corinthians 5:21). This amazing, privileged status that we have in Christ is hinted at earlier in the storyline. The prophet Isaiah writes of the servant:

> "Out of the anguish of his soul he shall see and be satisfied;
> by his knowledge shall the righteous one, my servant,
> *make many to be accounted righteous,*
> and he share bear their iniquities." (Isaiah 53:11)

Jesus is the true Israel, God's chosen one. He is the individual seed of the woman and individual descendant of Abraham. All who belong to him, by faith, all who are "in Christ" are, therefore, the corporate Israel, the corporate seed of the woman, the corporate, spiritual descendants of Abraham, as the New Testament teaches.

We'll come back to what this important biblical relationship between the corporate group and an individual representative means for our understanding of persecution later in the chapter but, in the verses we have focused on, Matthew gives us one more pointer to the way Jesus fulfils God's promises.

When Herod realises he has been tricked by the wise men, he orders the slaughter of all the young male children in Bethlehem: his desperate way of trying to carry out his plan to destroy the Messiah. Matthew adds:

> "Then was fulfilled what was spoken by the prophet Jeremiah:
> 'A voice was heard in Ramah,
>   weeping and loud lamentation,
>   Rachel weeping for her children;
>   she refused to be comforted,
>   because they are no more.'"
>   (Matthew 2:17-18)

Matthew's quotation comes from Jeremiah 31:15. It is important to understand Jeremiah's use of imagery, if we are to grasp Matthew's point. Ramah, a few miles north of Jerusalem on the way to Bethel, is the place the people were made to march through on the way to exile (Jeremiah 40:1). It is also, most likely, the place where Rachel was buried many years earlier (Genesis 35:16-19).

We will sometimes refer flippantly to someone "turning in their grave". In not dissimilar fashion, Jeremiah is depicting the long-dead Rachel "weeping in her tomb" at the sight of her people being marched off to Babylon.

And yet Jeremiah 31 is, on the whole, a chapter full of hope! In the very next verse (after the verse Matthew quotes) we read: "Thus says the Lord: 'Keep your voice from weeping, and your eyes from tears...'" (Jeremiah 31:16).

In the short term, this hope meant the promise that the people would return from exile (Jeremiah 31:17-22). Ultimately, however, hope was expressed in the famous declaration that God would one day make a new covenant with his people (Jeremiah 31:31-34). This he has done in and through his Son, Jesus Christ. So when we fast-forward to the events at the beginning of Matthew's Gospel, we might say that, in the short term, Herod's atrocity in Bethlehem was indeed a cause for weeping – but God was working through his chosen Messiah, whom he had preserved, to bring his promises to fulfilment!

We have already seen in earlier chapters how the two historic events that lay behind the quotations from Hosea and Jeremiah – the Exodus and the return from exile – also form part of the big-picture storyline that is pointing to Jesus. Both depict God redeeming his people. In doing so, both anticipate a yet greater work of redemption that God will accomplish to fulfil his promises.

VICTORY IN CONFLICT

How, then, did Jesus bring about this greater work of redemption, and so fulfil the promises of God?

The answer to that question is, of course, found at the cross. In one sense, it is an answer that seems so obvious to us that it scarcely seems worthwhile asking. But that's because we have read (and know for ourselves) the whole story!

In the time of Jesus, though, there was great expectation among many of the Jews that the Messiah, when he came, would bring about victory in the way the historic King David had been victorious: through military conflict. In Jesus' day, Israel was occupied by the Romans; before that they had suffered under the Greeks. 'Messianic hope', perhaps not surprisingly, had crystallised into a popular vision that involved kicking the occupying Gentiles out of the land.

Salvation at the cross

And yet for those with eyes to see, the storyline itself had always suggested something bigger, deeper, more significant and long-lasting than this. Faithful old Simeon, to whom the Lord had spoken about the coming of the Messiah, said, when he saw the baby Jesus:

> "Lord, now you are letting your servant depart in peace,
>   according to your word;
> for my eyes have seen your salvation
>   that you have prepared in the presence of all peoples,
> a light for revelation to the Gentiles,
>   and for glory to your people Israel."
>
> (Luke 2:29-32)

In the opening scene of his Gospel, Matthew reports the angel of the Lord saying to Joseph of Mary: "She will bear a son, and you shall call his name Jesus, for he will save his people from their *sins*" (Matthew 1:21). From their sins, note, not merely from human enemies.

Isaiah's depiction of the Suffering Servant had focused on suffering that would atone for sin. The sacrificial system instituted in Moses' day established the principle of a substitutionary sacrifice for sin. And God's first promise-in-judgement was made in the context of an original sin that separated mankind from God: a seed of the woman would conquer – but not without suffering himself. All of this points us to the suffering of Jesus Christ on the cross.

When Jesus began to prepare his disciples for this, Peter tried to dissuade him from even contemplating such an outcome. During and immediately after Jesus' death, the disciples are represented in the Gospels as confused, despondent and defeated. The resurrection changed all that, of course. And beyond the day of Pentecost, they proclaimed in Jesus' death and resurrection a *victory:* a victory over sin, death and evil. A victory in the biggest and most significant conflict of them all: a conflict that goes right back to the Garden. And this brings us back to the actions of King Herod.

Many a Christmas sermon has been preached on the different reactions to Jesus seen in the story of the wise men's visit. Some have even employed "apt alliteration's artful aid" to speak of the *apathy* of the priests, the *anger* of Herod and the *adoration* of the magi! There is certainly deep irony in the fact that it is foreign Gentiles who respond positively to the Messiah.

Herod's violent reaction in having the male children of Bethlehem killed is reminiscent of the Pharaoh's attempt to exterminate the Hebrews in Moses' day (Exodus 1:8-22). Both events point us further back to Genesis 3 and the declaration that the serpent would bruise the heel of the seed of the woman. Herod's reaction reminds us of this age-long conflict, and so prepares us for what Christ would experience later in life.

We have seen that the fulfilment of God's promises involves the defeat of evil and the serpent through a seed of the woman, who will be a descendant of Abraham, who will come from the tribe of Judah, and who will be a royal son of David. Each facet of these promises points us to Jesus and the gospel. And yet, as the storyline reaches its climax, the New Testament reveals an extra layer to the fulfilment itself.

Already, but not yet

On the surface, Jesus' resurrection would lay claim to be another 'happy ever after' moment, akin to what we noted with Solomon's Temple in a previous chapter. Surely *this* is now the end of the story? Yes, Jesus has suffered but he has been raised. He has won. From an Old Testament perspective, resurrection meant the end of the story. Final victory. And yet, here we are, two thousand years on, still struggling with sin, still living in a less-than-perfect world, still conscious of the existence of evil. Moreover, the very existence and purpose of the book you are now reading is to examine, and to understand, biblically, why Christians are still persecuted and therefore how we should respond. So, if Christ's death and resurrection constituted the moment of victory, why is our world still the way it is?

The answer lay with what theologians commonly refer to as the already-not-yet tension of the New Testament. *Already* Jesus has the victory. Nothing else need – or can – be done, or accomplished, to make more certain the eternal salvation of all who belong to him by faith. But *not yet* have we seen the full, final consummation of that victory. That which the Old Testament prophets envisaged, from afar, as a single event, we now know to be something more complicated, for it encompasses two events: Christ's first coming to accomplish the work of salvation on the cross, and his return as the triumphant judging, reigning Lord of all. We live between those two events, in something of an "overlap of the ages" (to use another common phrase). The finale, the plot resolution – which is Christ's coming, to fulfil all of God's promises – has, as it were, been stretched out over a period of history. The apostles saw the last days not as something in a long-distant future but as having begun, as a result of Jesus' death and resurrection. Mankind has been living in the last days these past two thousand years.

The coming of Jesus Christ to fulfil all of God's promises has constituted a sequence of events that we might describe as suffering now, glory after. And, crucially, Jesus calls his people to follow him in this. After rebuking Peter for attempting to bypass the need for the cross, we hear Jesus declare:

> "If anyone would come after me, let him deny himself and take up his cross and follow me. For whoever would save his life will lose it, but whoever loses his life for my sake and the gospel's will save it."
>
> (Mark 8:34-35)

This is the reality of the age in which we live as followers of Jesus. Christians suffer for following Jesus and for preaching the gospel. And yet, we do still (already) have the victory!

Revelation 12

One important passage that helps us see how both of these things can be true is Revelation 12. In this chapter, the curtain is pulled back to reveal the heavenly, spiritual – indeed cosmic – reality and import of Christ's first coming – but also the implications it has for his followers in the age in which we live. You might find it helpful to read Revelation 12 at this point.

The events in this chapter are shaped by two great signs that John sees in this section of the revelation being given to him: a woman who is pregnant (Revelation 12:2) and a great red dragon, who, rather gruesomely, is intent on devouring her child as soon as it is born (Revelation 12:3-4). The child, we are told, is destined to "rule the nations with a rod of iron" (Revelation 12:5). This is a clear allusion to the anointed one in Psalm 2:9. From the ground we have already covered in the overall storyline, we can say this is evidently Jesus himself. Does that mean that the woman is therefore Mary? Well, not exactly. The imagery in Revelation 12 suggests more than a literal, individual woman. It would be more helpful to say that the pregnant woman represents the Messianic community, or people of God; a people from which the Messiah comes but which, at the same time, comes into being through the Messiah!

As far as the child is concerned, we are simply told that he "was caught up to God and to his throne" (Revelation 12:5). The birth, life, death, resurrection and ascension of Jesus are covered in one verse! What about the dragon?

John's vision seems to cover the same ground twice (Revelation 12:1-6 and then Revelation 12:7-17; for support of this view compare what happens to the woman in verse 6 and verse 14). As he steps further back to see the cosmic events surrounding the coming of this child John tells us: "And the great dragon was thrown down, that ancient serpent, who is called the devil and Satan, the deceiver of the whole world – he was thrown down to the earth…" (Revelation 12:9). So the dragon is Satan; he is the serpent from Genesis 3!

Notice that *after* what appears to be his defeat – the dragon goes on fighting! In verse 13 he pursues the woman. The woman is preserved somehow, and so then we read: "Then the dragon became furious with the woman and went off to make war on the rest of her offspring, on those who keep the commandments of God and hold to the testimony of Jesus" (Revelation 12:17).

The imagery in this vision highlights two themes that we need to bear in mind as we seek to understand the significance of the persecution of Christians in this present age.

First, *this is an age of spiritual conflict.* A vision which features a woman, her offspring and a serpent is clearly intended to remind us of the events in the Garden of Eden in Genesis 3. Here is the crux of that enmity referred to in Genesis 3:15, as the serpent and all who are aligned with him wage war against the seed of the woman. But the child "who is to rule the nations with a rod of iron" has been "caught up to God and to his throne"

(Revelation 12:5). So who does the serpent/dragon attack? The corporate seed of the woman ("the rest of her offspring")!

But, second, *this is an age in which Christ already has the victory!* Although the dragon's intent is to devour the child, his purposes are thwarted. He is described, in verse 8, as being "defeated". How has this victory come about? The imagery of the dragon being "thrown down" ought to remind us, perhaps, of the language Jesus himself used, shortly before his crucifixion, as well as John's comment on its significance:

> "'Now is the judgement of this world: now will the ruler of this world be cast out. And I, when I am lifted up from the earth, will draw all people to myself.' He said this to show by what kind of death he was going to die." (John 12:31-33)

The seed of the woman who would crush the serpent and his seed; the descendant of Abraham through whom we would be blessed; the son of David who would establish God's kingdom and bring in the reign of peace: this is Jesus Christ, whose victory, as the imagery of Revelation 12 suggests, is seen to have taken place at the cross. As we noted earlier, the cross, according to the New Testament's teaching, is the place not only of atonement, but also of the victory over the spiritual powers of evil.

This, therefore, is an age in which Christ already has the victory. And yet, this is an age of spiritual conflict. At first glance, those two concepts seem contradictory: they appear to grate. But a biblical theology, big-picture reading of the storyline, in which we understand both the 'already' and the 'not yet' of that victory, encourages us to hold those themes in tension.

To do so is to take a huge step towards understanding – and, therefore, beginning to respond appropriately to – the persecution of Christians in our world today.

OUR RESPONSE TO THE STORY SO FAR

Biblical theology encourages us to follow the big picture of the Bible; to recognise a coherent storyline in God's revelation. Like all storylines it has progression; there is what we have called a trajectory, with later events and promises building on, and filling out the picture of earlier events and promises. From the outset we suggested that this is how the Bible itself teaches us to read, interpret and apply the Bible today.

In Chapters 3 to 5 of this book, we traced the development of God's promise, from the initial good news in Genesis 3 that God will overcome evil, through the promise of blessing made to Abraham, to the promise of a king whose kingdom will endure forever. At each of these stages we saw how the storyline can be tracked through to Jesus and the gospel.

But at the same time, we also saw the ongoing presence of conflict, a flipside to those promises, as those who oppose God seek to defy him by the way they respond to what he has said, done and promised.

Now, we arrive at the coming of Jesus himself. The opening of Matthew's Gospel sets the tone, introducing Jesus in a way that makes clear he stands at the end of this great biblical storyline. All of God's promises point to him and are fulfilled in him.

And yet conflict is still present in the story. Herod's hostile reaction serves to remind us that the serpent and his seed seek to defy God's purposes. Ironically, we might say, it is in the apparent *defeat* of the cross that Jesus accomplishes the victory for which he came. In his Pentecost Day sermon, Peter acknowledged that this was all in the hand of God:

> "This Jesus, delivered up according to the definite plan and foreknowledge of God, you crucified and killed by the hands of lawless men."   (Acts 2:23)

This should come as no surprise, for in that very first promise

God declares that it is he who will put enmity between the woman and the serpent, and between their respective seed. And if the seed of the woman will conquer, it will not be without suffering himself.

We still await the consummation of that victory, in the final judgement and the making of all things new in the New Heavens and New Earth.

In the meantime, John's vision in Revelation 12 has reminded us what this will mean. We should recognise three things:

1. *Christians are caught up in a battle.*

Although the conflict anticipated in Genesis 3:15 and seen throughout the Old Testament storyline comes to a head in the cross of Christ, Revelation 12 suggests the battle continues! The seed of the serpent continues to bite the seed of the woman! Satan is a defeated foe – but a defiant foe. In fact, it is the very certainty of his defeat which prompts his rage! John, writing *after* "the salvation and the power and the kingdom of our God and the authority of his Christ have come" (Revelation 12:10), declares:

> "Therefore, rejoice, O heavens and you who dwell in them! But woe to you, O earth and sea, for the devil has come down to you in great wrath, because he knows that his time is short!" (Revelation 12:12)

One helpful analogy often used by preachers to illustrate this is the relationship between the D-Day landings of June 1944 and the actual end of the Second World War the following year. The success of the D-Day operation effectively signalled the beginning of the end. Nevertheless, Hitler's Nazi war machine continued fighting – and many more bloody battles took place before the end finally came. Such analogies are never perfect, of course: Christ's victory on the cross makes the ultimate end far more certain than did that offensive in the summer of 1944. But, nevertheless, it makes the point: as Hitler fought on, though facing defeat, so does the evil one.

Not only is his time short, but his sphere of influence is always limited by the sovereign hand of God. This is seen in the protection of the woman (Revelation 12:14) for "a time, and times, and half a time", a somewhat mysterious phrase, which seems to be identified with the 1,260 days of verse 6, and which probably refers to the entire, unknown period of time that constitutes this present age before Christ returns.

2. *Christians will suffer.*

John tells us that, in his wrath and fury, the dragon, though defeated, defiantly makes war on the corporate seed of the woman (see Revelation 12:17).

One might argue that that last sentence sums up a biblical understanding of the ultimate spiritual reason for the persecution of Christians in this present age.

Mention of the corporate seed of the woman reminds us of that important biblical principle we touched on in the first part of this chapter (and earlier in the book): that is, the relationship between the corporate group and the individual representative.

We said earlier that this key concept helps us understand the Bible's teaching on the universal nature of sin, on how Christ's death benefits us personally, and the assurance we have of being declared righteous before God. But it also helps us understand persecution. Because we are "in Christ", we not only suffer *for* Christ: there is a sense in which we also suffer *with* him (Romans 8:17). Not that we share with him in atoning for sin, but that we experience the world's hatred of Christ and its rejection of God's promises, which in turn stems from the enmity of the serpent.

This clarifies and deepens our understanding and appreciation of Jesus' words at the Last Supper – the words which began this book:

> "If the world hates you, know that it has hated me before it hated you. If you were of the world, the world would love you as its own; but because you are not of the world, but I chose you out of the world, therefore the world hates you." (John 15:18-19)

There may be many things in this life which take us by surprise. If we have a big-picture understanding of the Bible and its storyline, persecution should not be one of them. In the New Testament the apostles speak of persecution as something to be expected. It seems they taught it to new Christians as part of what we might refer to as Christian basics – as we will see in the next chapter.

3. Christians have the victory!

In saying that Christians have the victory, we have to recognise, of course, that this is not what the world might recognise as victory. Christ's victory came through the apparent defeat of the cross (albeit coupled with his resurrection) – and our victory is in him. The victory we have in Christ is not short term – although, praise God, he does give us short-term victories at times. He does bless us in this earthly life, as we acknowledged in Chapter 4. As far as our main theme is concerned, that means there are times, thankfully, when God protects his people from persecution, or delivers pastors who have been imprisoned for their faith. We praise God when he does these things in response to our prayers, and it inspires us (or should) to go on praying that God will continue to be at work in this way.

But whether or not God acts for us in these short-term ways, our victory is a long-term one. It has the perspective of the apostle Paul:

> "If then you *have been* raised with Christ, seek the things that are above, where Christ is seated at the right hand of God. Set your minds on things that are

above, not on things that are on earth. For you *have* died, and your life *is* hidden with Christ in God. When Christ who is your life appears, then you also *will* appear with him in glory." (Colossians 3:1-4)

Notice the tenses Paul employs. Notice what is already true if you are in Christ. Notice the certainty it gives for the future.

In Revelation 12 this is how John describes those who belong to Christ, those whom the dragon would seek to assault:

"And they have conquered him by the blood of the Lamb and by the word of their testimony, for they loved not their lives even unto death." (Revelation 12:11)

Our victory over evil is through all that Christ has already accomplished for us on the cross. And it is maintained and lived out by a faithful witness to the gospel[21] - even to the point of being willing to suffer for that gospel; for Christ walked a path of suffering that leads to glory - and he calls his people to do the same.

Revelation 12, we might say, tells it as it is. Its peek behind the curtain reveals the spiritual realities that lay behind what we see with our eyes. But it is not, of course, the end of the story! Another benefit of a big-picture reading of Scripture is in knowing how it all ends. In the same book, John reminds us of a coming day when "[God] will wipe away every tear from [his people's] eyes, and death shall be no more, neither shall there be mourning, nor crying, nor pain anymore, for the former things have passed away" (Revelation 21:4).

---

[21] "The word of their *testimony*" here doesn't mean what we tend to mean by "giving our testimony", that is, telling our personal story of coming to faith. The 'testimony' is the word of their *witness*: in other words, their testimony is the content of the gospel, the message about Christ, not us!

Acts 13:49-50

"And the word of the Lord was spreading through the whole region. But the Jews incited the devout women of high standing and the leading men of the city, stirred up persecution against Paul and Barnabas, and drove them out of their district."

7. The Promise *proclaimed*

"WHERE was God?" That's the pain-filled question we sometimes want to cry out in the face of disaster, tragedy or evil in our world.

It is a question we may wrestle with when we are confronted with the persecution of Christians for their faith in Christ. Behind it lay the thought that, if God is in control and if God is loving, it doesn't seem to make sense to us why he would allow his people to suffer.

At one level we can resign ourselves to acknowledging that we don't know why these things happen. We are not God. True – but does our big-picture, biblical theology reading of Scripture help us to see, and say, more than that?

In the last chapter, we saw that Jesus' coming into the world, to die on the cross for our sins and to rise again, is the climax of God's promises. He is the individual seed of the woman who would overcome the serpent and his seed – by suffering; He is the individual descendent of Abraham, through whom all kinds of people will be blessed by God; He is the anointed Son of David, who will establish a kingdom of peace that will endure forever.

But if Jesus is the final plot resolution in God's storyline, who draws together and fulfils all the promises of the Old Testament, why is our world still the way it is? Why – in the context of this book's theme – do Christians still suffer for their faith and for their Christian witness?

We suggested that an answer lay in what is often referred to as the already-not-yet tension within the New Testament picture of history. What Old Testament prophets saw, from afar, simply as the End, the New Testament describes as an End that is stretched out over an unknown period of time: the time between Christ's first coming and his return in glory. We live in the overlap between what is 'already' and what is 'not yet'.

One illustration I heard many years ago helps describe this development from the Old into the New Testament. Imagine you are driving in a mountainous part of the country. You see, in the distance, a mountain peak. As your journey takes you nearer, you observe that it seems the mountain in question actually has two distinct peaks. The closer the winding road takes you, the further apart those two peaks appear to be until, finally, you realise the road you are travelling on is going to pass between them: they are, in fact, two separate mountains! And there comes a point in the journey when one is now behind you and one is still in front of you.

The trajectory of the Bible's storyline is rather like that. The hope and promise of the Old Testament is expanded and developed as it comes into its New Testament fulfilment. This is one reason why it is so important to develop a big-picture reading of Scripture: we can easily misinterpret earlier parts of the story if we fail to see how they are fleshed out in later parts of the story.

This already-not-yet perspective can be illustrated by considering Jesus' teaching on the kingdom (often regarded as the central theme of his preaching). When we study the Gospels, we see there are times when Jesus claims the kingdom *has come*, or is present, or is in people's midst (eg Luke 10:9, 11:20, 17:21). In each case Jesus implies the kingdom has come because he has come. We might say the kingdom has come because the King has come. Moreover, Jesus teaches that the kingdom is entered by responding to him (eg Luke 18:16-17; 18:22-25).

And yet there are also times when Jesus speaks of the kingdom as something *future*, or at least as something that has a future dimension (eg Luke 19:11-27; 22:18). In one sense, speaking of the kingdom as a future event would have been more in line with Old Testament expectation; what was more radical was the claim that the hoped-for kingdom of God was being made manifest in Jesus himself!

So what does the kingdom of God look like during this already-not-yet time in which we now live? This is clearly an important question, and not least for helping us understand and respond to the persecution of Christians.

In many respects, the book of Acts serves to answer these sorts of questions. Both volumes of Luke's writings, both the book of Acts and Luke, are addressed to a man called Theophilus. In each case Luke's introductions reveal much about why he wrote. His Gospel, he tells us, is an ordered, eyewitness account of the life, death and resurrection of Jesus, produced so that his reader(s) "may have certainty concerning the things you have been taught" (Luke 1:4). The Gospel ends (as we saw back in Chapter 2) with strong, post-resurrection teaching from Jesus, emphasising that all of God's Old Testament promises have been fulfilled in him (Luke 24).

Luke begins volume two by declaring: "In the first book, O Theophilus, I have dealt with all that Jesus *began* to do and teach, until the day when he was taken up..." (Acts 1:1-2. As many commentators have pointed out, this strongly implies that Luke is about to deal with all that Jesus *continued* to do, as the ascended Lord. In a powerful and persuasive study of the book of Acts, Alan J Thompson writes:

> "Luke is writing to provide reassurance to believers about the nature of the events surrounding Jesus' life, death, resurrection, the spread of the message about Jesus, and the nature of God's people following Jesus' ascension. He is providing assurance that these events really are the work of God, that God really has been accomplishing his purposes, that Jesus really is who he said he was, and that believers in Jesus really are the true people of God. All of this is especially

important in the light of the rejection and persecution faced by these believers..."[22]

Note, in particular, that final sentence. The book of Acts helps us to see that the last days (which we defined earlier as encompassing the entire period between Christ's first and second comings) will be characterised by gospel preaching, through which the kingdom grows, *and* – at the same time – by opposition to that gospel from the world.

PREACHING THE PROMISE

Luke's account in the book of Acts includes, at regular intervals, comments about the spread and growth of the word of God (see, for example, Acts 6:7; 12:24; 19:20). This is clearly a major theme in the book, as we see the gospel spreading from its original roots in Jerusalem to different parts of the known world. If, as we suggested above, the book of Acts is illustrating the work that the risen Lord Jesus *continued* to do (after his ascension), then that work, of building his kingdom, comes through the preaching of God's word, and the calling of people to faith in Christ himself.

Preaching the resurrection

A number of sermons or speeches are recorded in considerable detail during the course of the book of Acts. One observable feature of these proclamations is the emphasis on the resurrection of Jesus.

This doesn't mean the cross wasn't important – either for the apostles who preached, or for Luke who wrote. In both their preaching and their writing, the apostles Peter and Paul (the two most prominent preachers in Acts) spell out clearly the centrality of Christ's saving work on the cross, in terms of bearing our sin

---

[22] Alan J Thompson, *The Acts of the Risen Lord Jesus*, New Studies in Biblical Theology 27 (Nottingham: Apollos, 2011), pp.19,20

and its consequences. Likewise, across his two volumes, Luke demonstrates the same understanding of Jesus' death as a substitutionary sacrificial work, and a means of forgiveness and mercy for everyone who submits to Jesus Christ as Lord and Saviour. Nevertheless, the emphasis on the resurrection in the speeches of Acts is clear to see. Why?

In the resurrection of Jesus, the age to come has entered into our present age! In other words, the resurrection of Jesus is absolutely central to that already-not-yet perspective we have been considering, and which the book of Acts as a whole is going to demonstrate.

As we noted earlier, orthodox, old covenant Jewish belief and hope were in a physical resurrection at the very end of the age. We see an illustration of this in John's account of the raising of Lazarus. When Jesus promises Martha that her brother will rise again, Martha replies: "I know that he will rise again in the resurrection on the last day" (John 11:24). What a wonderfully sound, credal statement (from an Old Testament perspective)! But notice that in his reply Jesus doesn't simply say, "No, Martha, I mean now: I'm going to bring him back to life now!" Rather, he says,

> "I am the resurrection and the life. Whoever believes in me, though he die, yet shall he live, and everyone who lives and believes in me shall never die."
> (John 11:25-26)

Jesus' memorable statement focuses attention on himself, rather than on the condition of Lazarus (or even on the miracle Jesus was about to perform to bring Lazarus back to life). That resurrection life in which Martha believed is to be found in and through Jesus! His resurrection, which is the climax of the Gospel accounts, assures us of this.

And so when, post ascension, the followers of Jesus begin the task of preaching and spreading the word of God, they do so on the understanding that the physical resurrection of Jesus from the dead is the beginning of the realisation, or fulfilment, of that Old Testament hope for the end.

In the final chapters of the book, as the apostle Paul is defending himself before various authorities, he declares on more than one occasion that he is on trial for his hope in the resurrection of the dead (Acts 23:6; 24:15; 24:21). But what is it that separates him from his Jewish accusers? In his final defence, he spells it out:

> "I stand here testifying both to small and great, saying nothing but what the prophets and Moses said would come to pass: that the Christ must suffer and that, *by being the first to rise from the dead*, he would proclaim light both to our people and to the Gentiles."
>
> (Acts 26:22-23)

Alan J Thompson says of this statement:

> "Here, finally and climactically, Luke includes Paul's clarification of what he has meant throughout his earlier defences by stating that he is on trial for 'the resurrection of the dead' (plural). Jesus' resurrection is an end-time eschatological event that has already taken place in this age. As in Acts 4:2, to proclaim Jesus' resurrection was to proclaim the introduction (already in this age) of the eschatological blessings reserved for the resurrection age (at the end of this age) for all those who belong to Jesus."[23]

Jesus' resurrection is, therefore, the 'firstfruits' (as Paul describes it in 1 Corinthians 15:20-23) because his bodily resurrection anticipates, and guarantees, what will be the

---

[23] Thompson, *The Acts of the Risen Lord Jesus*, p.81

experience for every believer at the end of this age. His bodily resurrection is, as we suggested above, the age to come breaking into this present age. We are seeing a first glimpse of the age to come in the bodily resurrection of Jesus.

This was what made its reality such a crucial event for the apostles as they began proclaiming the gospel.

CAUGHT IN THE CONFLICT

Christ's resurrection, then, was the beginning of the end. So what should we expect to see in these last days? Luke's account in the book of Acts emphasises the spread of the word of the Lord. As the message about Jesus Christ's death and resurrection is proclaimed by his servants, God does what only God can do: he works, by his Holy Spirit, to bring people to conviction, repentance and faith. In this way people from all nations come to share in the victory of the seed of the woman. In this way people from all nations experience the blessing that was promised through the individual offspring of Abraham.

But that is only part of the picture presented in the book of Acts.

There is the 'not yet' in what we have been calling the already-not-yet tension of the New Testament. Already Christ has won the victory, but not yet has every knee bowed and every tongue confessed that Jesus Christ is Lord, to the glory of God the Father (Philippians 2:10-11). As we have seen in the previous chapter, the serpent's time may be short (Revelation 12:12), but it is a time of making war on the corporate seed of the woman (Revelation 12:17). Persecution is not, by any means, the only way the serpent and his seed oppose Christ and the gospel – but it is certainly one significant way.

This quickly becomes apparent in the book of Acts. In almost every chapter, hostile opposition stands alongside the spread of God's word. In the Temple story of chapters three and four, Peter and John are arrested for "proclaiming in Jesus the resurrection from the dead" (Acts 4:2). In chapter five, the apostles are arrested again, as "more than ever believers were added to the Lord, multitudes of both men and women" (Acts 5:14). In chapter six, Stephen is seized and then, after defending the gospel in chapter seven, martyred. In chapter eight, "a great persecution" arises against the growing infant church (Acts 8:1) but the word continues to be preached. In chapter nine, Saul – prior to his conversion – is "still breathing threats and murder against the disciples of the Lord" (Acts 9:1), and so on.

Indeed, when Saul, or Paul (as he would come to be known), *is* converted, God's declaration about the future course of his life is itself a testimony to the way these two themes – the spread of the gospel and the opposition of the world – will stand side by side. In response to Ananias' trepidation (about approaching a man who has, thus far, been an enemy of the gospel), Luke reports:

> "But the Lord said to him, 'Go, for he is a chosen instrument of mine to carry my name before the Gentiles and kings and the children of Israel. For I will show him how much he must suffer for the sake of my name." (Acts 9:15-16)

One paradigmatic section of the book of Acts that amply demonstrates both aspects of this already-not-yet tension is Paul's first missionary journey, recorded in Acts 13 and 14. As we shall see, the climax of this journey also gives us strong biblical pointers towards how we should be responding to the needs of persecuted Christians around the world today.

Paul's first missionary journey (Acts 13 & 14)

Paul and Barnabas are commissioned and sent out by their home church, in Syrian Antioch (Acts 13:1-3). The mission starts on the island of Cyprus (Acts 13:4-12), where they proclaim the word of God – but are, at the same time, opposed by the false prophet, Bar-Jesus (also known as Elymas). Paul's response is striking:

> "You son of the devil, you enemy of all righteousness, full of all deceit and villainy, will you not stop making crooked the straight paths of the Lord?"   (Acts 13:10)

Our modern sensibilities might lead us to conclude that this is a little excessive or insulting! "Steady on, Paul," we might say, "there's no need to offend the man!" But is this not the language of Genesis 3? The seed of the serpent is once again opposing the seed of the woman. Paul declares that, because of this opposition, Elymas will be blinded for a period. Luke adds: "Immediately mist and *darkness* fell upon him..." (Acts 13:11). In the Bible darkness is often a sign of God's curse. "Cursed are you," the Lord had said to the serpent (Genesis 3:14).

After sailing across to Perga, they arrive in Pisidian Antioch (not to be confused with the Antioch they set out from). Here Luke records, at length, a synagogue sermon by Paul (Acts 13:16-41). This sermon is a wonderful example of the kind of big-picture, biblical theology reading of Scripture we have been following in this book. Paul traces God's promise from the Exodus to David and then declares: "Of this man's offspring God has brought to Israel a Saviour, Jesus, as he promised" (Acts 13:23). Paul focuses on Christ's resurrection, as a fulfilment of God's promise to his anointed one in Psalms 2 and 16, and, as the logical conclusion to this summary of God's story, makes the gospel appeal, declaring:

> "Let it be known to you therefore, brothers, that through this man forgiveness of sins is proclaimed to you, and by him everyone who believes is freed from everything from which you could not be freed by the Law of Moses."   (Acts 13:38-39)

And the response? Some were willing to hear more (Acts 13:42); some appear to have believed there and then (13:43). Some, however, mount a verbal attack on Paul the following week

(Acts 13:45). Those whom God is calling rejoice (Acts 13:48); others, however, "stirred up persecution against Paul and Barnabas, and drove them out of their district" (Acts 13:50). Notice how the reference to persecution is preceded by one of those summary statements of Luke: "And the word of the Lord was spreading throughout the whole region" (Acts 13:49).

Driven from Antioch, Paul and Barnabas go on to Iconium. Again they preach the gospel (Luke doesn't feel the need to record the sermon in detail). Again we are told "a great number of both Jews and Greeks believed" (Acts 14:1) while, again, others oppose them and even seek to stone them (Acts 14:5). The biblical pattern we have observed from the beginning is continuing.

They move on to Lystra, where their gospel ministry is misunderstood, more than opposed (Acts 14:8-18). However, we then read:

> "But Jews came from Antioch and Iconium, and having persuaded the crowds, they stoned Paul and dragged him out of the city..." (Acts 14:19)

The opponents of Paul and his gospel won't let go! The queue of people pursuing him is getting longer the more places he visits.[24]

Having recovered from the stoning, Paul travels on with Barnabas to Derbe, where they again preach the gospel and make "many disciples" (Acts 14:21).

Growth and suffering

At this point Paul's journey has come – almost – to a logical conclusion. He has completed something of a round-trip. But

---

[24] The New Testament Greek words usually translated 'to persecute' or 'persecution' have a root meaning of 'pursuing'. Paul's experience at Lystra – where opponents from Antioch and Iconium had literally *pursued* him – could be described as the archetypal example of persecution!

before we go on to consider what Paul does next, we should pause and consider what his experiences during this highly significant first missionary journey teach us.

We have seen the gospel preached and people won for Christ. Alongside this we have seen people opposing the gospel, to the point of persecuting those who proclaim it.

We should take care not to be overly simplistic in the conclusions we draw from this. We should not, on the one hand, measure a church's faithfulness to the gospel by the extent to which it experiences persecution. Nor should we assume that a certain degree of opposition and persecution will automatically and inextricably lead to some measurably corresponding degree of gospel spread and growth. Life is not that simple and uniform. As two thousand years of church history demonstrate, it *is* possible at times to see marked gospel growth without severe persecution, and it *is* possible at times to see persecution stifle and weaken the church's gospel witness.

On the other hand, we should not downplay or ignore the prominence given to persecution and opposition in the book of Acts – and, in particular, its experience *alongside* the spread of the gospel. Paul House has argued that Acts has no purpose, no plot, no structure and no history without suffering.

> "Certainly suffering is a major force in the gospel's expansion. It is a rare thing for the Way to spread without it. Various summaries in the text point to this conclusion (8:4; 9:16; 14:22; 20:22-24; 21:13; etc.), as does the flow of the book's last nine chapters. Certainly the gospel moves, but never without pain. Thus the Church needs a theological understanding and practical application of how to deal with this everyday reality."[25]

---

[25] Paul R House, 'Suffering and the Purpose of Acts', *Journal of the Evangelical Theological Society* 33/3 (September 1990), pp.321, 326

What Paul's experiences during that first missionary journey *do* undoubtedly demonstrate is that we can expect both of these things to be occurring during the last days in which we live, during the already-not-yet time between Christ's ascension and his return.

We should expect to see the word of God spreading; indeed, we should be praying and labouring for this. We should rejoice whenever we see those who are "appointed to eternal life" hearing the gospel and believing.

But we should also expect to see the rebellious world continuing to rail against that gospel, to see the serpent and his seed 'bruising the heel' of the corporate seed of the woman. As we have already remarked, persecution is not the only manifestation of this opposition (false teaching *within* the church would be another) – but it is a significant one. A big-picture, biblical theology reading of the Scriptures helps us see that this is so. We should be prepared, and we should know how to respond.

At the end of his life's work, Paul (in what was probably his last letter) wrote to Pastor Timothy about what to expect and what to do after he had gone. At one point he comments:

> "You, however, have followed my teaching, my conduct, my aim in life, my faith, my patience, my love, my steadfastness, my persecutions and sufferings that happened to me at Antioch, at Iconium, and at Lystra..." (2 Timothy 3:10-11)

Commentators sometimes remark that Paul mentions those places because Timothy was himself converted at some point during that first missionary journey. Certainly it is true that when Paul returns to Derbe and Lystra on his second missionary journey, he meets Timothy who is, at that stage, already a believer (see Acts 16:1-2).

However, even if it transpires that Timothy *was* converted

during that time, I think there may be a further reason why Paul singles out those places from that ground-breaking mission.

Here he is, in prison, knowing that his life's work is at an end. He expects to be martyred soon (see 2 Timothy 4:6-8). He looks back over the years, back to the beginning of his missionary journeys. He knows, of course, that he has preached the gospel – and this short letter is full of encouragement to Timothy to do the same – but in these particular verses his focus is on the opposition he has faced. It is, perhaps, as though he is saying to Timothy: That's what it was like at the very beginning – *and, you know, that's what it continues to be like.*

As we've already remarked, this does not mean that persecution is manifested in a constant, uniform way: after all, even within the limited time-frame of that first missionary journey, Paul himself experienced opposition in different ways and to differing degrees of severity. Nevertheless, Paul seems to be stressing, these things are to be expected. We should expect to see opposition to Christ and the gospel. That Paul has this in mind seems to be reinforced by what he goes on to say in the very next verse:

> "Indeed, all who desire to live a godly life in Christ Jesus will be persecuted." (2 Timothy 3:12)

The word of God will continue to spread and, by God's grace, people will continue to come to faith in Christ as they hear the gospel. The world (behind which lies the serpent) will continue to oppose God's word – and will sometimes do this through the medium of outright persecution.

The book of Acts teaches us to see that this is what happens in the last days, as we live with the already-not-yet of God's purposes.

OUR RESPONSE TO THE STORY SO FAR

We have come a long way in our journey through the storyline of the Bible. With our goal of understanding, and of determining how to respond biblically, to persecution we have reached the age in which we now live, between the first and second comings of Christ.

We have followed God's promise through the different epochs of the Old Testament to its fulfilment in the life, death and resurrection of Jesus Christ. We have kept reminding ourselves that Jesus is the individual seed of the woman, the individual descendant of Abraham, and the individual Son of David. Every facet of God's promise is realised in him.

But with Christ's resurrection (and ascension), the End of all things has not come upon this world at once. The age to come has broken in with the bodily resurrection of Jesus, but we live with an already-not-yet dimension to God's promise. We have still to see the final consummation of the promises that Christ has already fulfilled.

Because of this we see still the conflict engendered by those promises, as the serpent and his seed oppose God and his anointed one. And because Christ has been "caught up to God and to his throne" (Revelation 12:5), his body on earth – the church – experiences that opposition, in its spiritual union with its Lord and Saviour.

"If the world hates you, know that it has hated me before it hated you," said Jesus at the Last Supper (John 15:18). We know this to be true, even today. A big-picture, biblical theology reading of the Scriptures helps us to understand why.

So what is our response? How should the church of Jesus Christ respond to the persecution of Christians in the world today?

The end of Paul's first missionary journey

We haven't yet quite finished our reading of Paul's first

missionary journey. We left him in Derbe, having almost completed a round-trip from Syrian Antioch. What happens next is hugely significant for us.

> "When they had preached the gospel to that city and had made many disciples, they returned to Lystra and to Iconium and to Antioch, strengthening the souls of the disciples, encouraging them to continue in the faith, and saying that through many tribulations we must enter the kingdom of God." (Acts 14:21-22)

Before we look at these verses in detail, let's pause to consider what Paul did. If you look at a map of Paul's first missionary journey, it is apparent that, from Derbe, the obvious direction for Paul to have taken at this point would have been to have headed east. This would have been the quickest, safest, easiest way back to Syrian Antioch as it would have followed a well-known Roman trade road. Indeed, Paul would have been familiar with this road for it passed through his original home town of Tarsus, in Cilicia.

I suspect most of us will have had that experience in life when we reach a point where we 'just want to get home'. However significant, or even enjoyable, a trip has been, once our mind begins to contemplate getting back, we naturally want to do so, as quickly and painlessly as possible!

But Paul didn't return that way.

Instead, he took the long and difficult option. He deliberately retraced his steps. Not only would this have been a more arduous journey, it meant, of course, revisiting the very places where he had faced opposition. In Iconium they had attempted to stone him; in Lystra they had succeeded!

To appreciate this is to grasp the importance Paul attached to what he set out to do, as he revisited believers. Luke describes it in two ways: *strengthening* souls and *encouraging* them to persevere. The latter is linked, notably, to a realisation of the inevitability of opposition and persecution. Strengthening would have meant, first and foremost, teaching them from the word of God; discipling, in a full and proper biblical sense of that word.

Paul had experienced opposition in these places and would have assumed that the infant churches he left behind in those different towns would be facing the same kind of opposition. This deliberate act, in retracing his steps, becomes therefore very instructive for us in determining how we should seek to respond to persecution today.

This observation becomes even more marked, I believe, when we compare these verses with something Paul writes later in his ministry to the church in Thessalonica.

Paul's response to the persecution of Christians

Paul visited Thessalonica during his second missionary journey (Acts 17:1-9). Once again his gospel ministry leads some people to believe – and others to oppose, aggressively. The upshot is that he is encouraged by the believers there to leave by night for Berea (Acts 17:10).

By the time he writes to the church in Thessalonica, it is evident that the believers have been growing in their faith – and have quickly earned a reputation for zealously sharing the gospel with others (see 1 Thessalonians 1:2-10). However, despite all the positive signs of spiritual growth, Paul had evidently been sufficiently anxious about the level of opposition they were facing to despatch Timothy to visit them.

The letter is written after Timothy's return, and Paul is delighted that his assistant has come back with good news of how the Thessalonian Christians are doing (see 1 Thessalonians 3:6-8).

What interests us at this point, though, is Paul's description of what he had sent Timothy to do. It is helpful to compare it with the verses we have been looking at in Acts 14. In both cases the key words are highlighted in bold, with their New Testament Greek originals transliterated and italicised.

> "... **strengthening** (verb: *epi-steridzo*) the souls of the disciples, **encouraging** (verb: *parakaleo*) them to continue in the faith, and saying that through many **tribulations** (noun: *thlipsis*) we must enter the kingdom of God." (Acts 14:22)

> "... and we sent Timothy... to **establish** (verb: *steridzo*[26]) and **exhort** (verb: *parakaleo*) you in your faith, that no one be moved by these **afflictions** (noun: *thlipsis*). For you yourselves know that we are destined for this." (1 Thessalonians 3:2-3)

In Acts 14:22 Luke is describing what Paul did. In 1 Thessalonians 3:2 Paul is describing what he sent Timothy to do. In both cases the context is responding to the needs of Christians who were suffering persecution. The similarities are, I believe, striking.

I don't think it is going too far to suggest that, in our analysis of these two passages, we are seeing something of an apostolic model for responding to the persecution of Christians.

The already-not-yet dimensions of the last days in which we

---

[26] New Testament writers frequently employ what we call compound verbs, where a preposition is added to a verb. In Acts 14:22 *epi-steridzo* is a compound verb (I have added the hyphen to illustrate this). *Epi* as a word on its own has a range of meanings including things like 'on', 'upon' or 'over'. Sometimes a compound verb will have a different meaning to the simpler form, but often its use is stylistic, or for emphasis, as is the case here.

The verb *steridzo* (from 1 Thessalonians 3:2) occurs 13 times in the New Testament. On all but two occasions it has the meaning of 'strengthening', or 'establishing' someone (in their faith). The apostle Paul is the most frequent user of this verb. The compound form *epi-steridzo* occurs four times, all of which are in the book of Acts.

I note that the two occasions when *steridzo* has the slightly different meaning of 'fixing' or 'setting' occur in Luke's Gospel (9:51 and 16:26). This suggests to me that Luke preferred to use *epi-steridzo* when he was thinking of 'strengthening' someone in their faith.

The upshot of this, I believe, is there is no real difference between Luke's use of *epi-steridzo* and Paul's use of *steridzo*.

live make paramount the need to strengthen Christians and to encourage them to persevere in their faith. That sounds like a basic description of discipleship. Well, if so, discipleship needs to embrace the reality of opposition and persecution, given our big-picture, biblical theology reading of the Bible's storyline. Notice the way that, in both passages, Paul comments on the inevitability of persecution: he considers it something normal for the Christian. Indeed, from the comments in his letter to the Thessalonians, it appears Paul had taught this to new believers as part of what we might refer to as Christian basics: "For you yourselves know that we are destined for this. For when we were with you, we kept telling you beforehand that we were to suffer affliction..." (1 Thessalonians 3:3-4).

What this strengthening and encouraging of persecuted Christians will look like, in terms of programmes, projects and practical action, needs thinking through and fleshing out, according to the different contexts in which God's suffering people are living today. We will say a little more about that in our conclusion.

Prayer

One final point that needs mentioning in our reflections on the end of Paul's first missionary journey is prayer. Immediately after Luke's description of what Paul set out to do, as he retraced his steps, we read:

> "And when they had appointed elders for them in every church, with *prayer* and fasting they committed them to the Lord in whom they had believed."
> (Acts 14:23)

The work of strengthening and encouraging does not negate the supreme value of intercessory prayer – and vice versa.

Similarly, in the parallel passage we have referred to, from 1 Thessalonians, we note the place of prayer. After acknowledging the good news Timothy has brought back, Paul writes of his thanksgiving to God and of his earnest prayer that he might see them again (1 Thessalonians 3:9-10). Then he continues:

> "Now may our God and Father himself, and our Lord Jesus, direct our way to you, and may the Lord make you increase and abound in love for one another and for all, as we do for you, so that *he may establish* your hearts blameless in holiness before our God and Father, at the coming of our Lord Jesus with all his saints." (1 Thessalonians 3:11-13)

Notice that clause in my italics. Paul prays that God *may establish* them. This is the same verb (*steridzo*) that Paul had used in verse 2. He sent Timothy to establish them – and he prays that God will establish them. Both are important. As with the situation he faced at the end of his first missionary journey, so here the work of strengthening and encouraging does not negate the supreme value of intercessory prayer – and vice versa.

Living in the last days

A big-picture, biblical theology reading of the Bible's storyline leads us to see that God's promises have been fulfilled in the life, death and resurrection of Jesus Christ. In his saving work the End has begun.

But not yet has that fulfilment of God's promises been fully and finally consummated. For that we await the return of Christ. In Jesus' resurrection we catch a glimpse of the age to come. When he returns that glorious age is all we shall see.

And so, until then, we live in these in-between times, with what we have been referring to as this already-not-yet tension. For the church, it is a time for going into the world and making disciples of all nations, as Jesus' closing words in Matthew's Gospel direct us (Matthew 28:18-20). We do so knowing that Jesus has all authority in heaven and on earth.

But we also do so knowing that, in this short time, opposition to Christ and the gospel continues. The gospel advance is not without suffering. It is through many tribulations that we must enter the kingdom of God.

A robust, biblical Christianity must understand that tension – and how we are to respond. That will mean that in our concern for those who suffer for Christ we must seek to strengthen them, to encourage them to persevere, and to pray for them. As Paul later prayed in his second letter to those persecuted Thessalonians:

> "Now may our Lord Jesus Christ himself, and God our Father, who loved us and gave us eternal comfort and good hope through grace, *comfort* your hearts and *establish*[27] them in every good work and word."
>
> (2 Thessalonians 2:16-17)

---

[27] Another example of Paul using those two verbs, *parakaleo* and *steridzo*, side by side.

Revelation 22:1-5

"Then the angel showed me the river of the water of life, bright as crystal, flowing from the throne of God and of the Lamb through the middle of the street of the city; also, on either side of the river, the tree of life with its twelve kinds of fruit, yielding its fruit each month. The leaves of the tree were for the healing of the nations. No longer will there be anything accursed, but the throne of God and of the Lamb will be in it, and his servants will worship him. They will see his face, and his name will be on their foreheads. And night will be no more. They will need no light of lamp or sun, for the Lord God will be their light, and they will reign forever and ever."

8. The Promise *consummated*

A GOOD story keeps us reading to the end. And the end of a good story is itself important. If we have stayed with the plot for that long, we naturally want a satisfying end: one that draws everything together in a gratifying and rewarding conclusion.

The greatest of all storylines – *God's* story – provides us with the greatest-ever ending. It is an ending that depicts the final state and purpose of God's creation, and the final fruit of Christ's saving work. It is an ending full of radiant hope for Christ's people – which makes it an important part of the story for those who suffer for him at present.

The final vision of the age to come, in John's Revelation, occurs in the last two chapters of that majestic book. It is introduced as a vision of "a new heaven and a new earth" (Revelation 21:1), a phrase which reminds us of Old Testament prophetic hope for the future (see Isaiah 65:17-25; 66:22). At the same time, the imagery which then follows takes us further back in the story – right back to the beginning, in fact.

The Bible's bookends

John's description of the new heaven and new earth quickly becomes a description of a new Jerusalem (Revelation 21:2). And yet it is a city that is incomprehensively large[28] – and, moreover, is cuboid (Revelation 21:16)!

Old Testament imagery runs deep throughout the book of Revelation, and this final vision is no exception. The shape of

---

[28] 12,000 stadia would be nearly 1,400 miles – in each direction!

this city – and the pure gold of which it is made (Revelation 21:18) – reminds us of the Temple or, more precisely, the Holy of Holies within the Temple (see 1 Kings 6:20). At the same time, careful readers of God's story will detect imagery in this final vision clearly intended to recall the Garden of Eden. A river of life flows from the throne of God (Revelation 22:1) as a river had flowed out of Eden (Genesis 2:10); the tree of life is present – and although fallen Man had been barred from it (Genesis 3:22), now, it seems, its fruit can be eaten (Revelation 22:2). Moreover, there is an intimacy to God's presence that reflects how things were in the beginning (Revelation 21:3-4; 22:4; Genesis 2:19; 3:8).

Because of these similarities the opening and closing chapters of Scripture are sometimes referred to as the Bible's 'bookends'. Once again, a big-picture, biblical theology reading of Scripture helps us appreciate how the imagery of this final vision in Revelation relates to the beginning and, indeed, how it helps us understand the ultimate purpose of God's creation. And as we wrestle with the painful reality of persecution in this already-not-yet age, it is a vision that crystallises the certainty of the Christian hope.

WHEN PROMISE BECOMES REALITY

So, the new heaven and new earth is also the new Jerusalem, which is also a temple (or tabernacle: see Revelation 21:3), which is also reminiscent of the original Garden! That seems to be a fair way of summing up the complex imagery of Revelation 21 and 22. And yet, at the same time, John writes: "And I saw no temple in the city, for its temple is the Lord God the Almighty and the Lamb" (Revelation 21:22)! What are we meant to make of all of this? The dominant thought behind all of this imagery seems to be the presence of God.

God's presence in the Old Testament

In the Old Testament the Temple – and its predecessor, the Tabernacle – was identified as the place of God's presence. This reality is seen most graphically (as we saw in an earlier chapter) in the Lord's glory filling both Tabernacle and Temple on completion (Exodus 40:34-35 and 1 Kings 8:10-11). The Lord's presence was expressed by the holiness – and, therefore, the inaccessibility – of the most inner part of both Tabernacle and Temple, the Holy of Holies. This contained the Ark of the Covenant, which was considered to be the footstool of the Lord (1 Chronicles 28:2; see also similar Temple-related imagery in Psalms 99:1-5 and 132:1-7). It is the construction of Solomon's Temple that marks out the Jerusalem of his day as special – not the other way round! Here was the place God had chosen to locate his presence at that point in the storyline.

The Tabernacle was established in Moses' day, after God had saved Israel out of Egypt and had established his covenant with them at Mount Sinai. The amount of space devoted to the Tabernacle in the book of Exodus – both the instructions to build it and then the subsequent report of it being built – may seem long-winded to some modern readers of the Bible, but it gives some indication as to its importance to the storyline. That God desires to dwell with those he has established as his people is clearly an important theme. But what about before the Exodus?

It is possible that we can detect a prototype or anticipation of the Tabernacle in the sacred altars set up by the patriarchs Abraham, Isaac and Jacob. These are often built, or referred to, in the context of reaffirmations by God of his promises, or of one of the patriarchs calling on the Lord (see, for example, Genesis 12:7-8; 13:4; 26:25; 28:12-17).

But if the dominant concept behind the Tabernacle and Temple is the presence of the Lord, we should properly trace the theme right back to the Garden of Eden.

We began our journey through the storyline of the Bible at

Genesis 3 because it is here – in the light of rebellion by the man and the woman – that we hear the first promise of God, the promise uttered in the context of judgement on the serpent (Genesis 3:15).

But in order to understand fully the significance of John's final vision in the book of Revelation, we need to go back even before the Fall of Genesis 3, to the Garden of Genesis 2.

As a number of writers in recent years have demonstrated, a big-picture reading of Scripture leads us to view the Garden as the first Temple or perhaps, if we turn it the other way round, to see the later Tabernacle and Temple as localised expressions of what the Garden was meant to be and become.

So, for example, the Garden was entered from the east and, post-Fall, was guarded by cherubim (Genesis 3:24), just as the later Tabernacle and Temple were entered from the east and had depictions of cherubim (eg Exodus 25:18-22; 1 Kings 6:23-29); gold and onyx, present in the Garden (Genesis 2:12) are later used in Temple decoration (Exodus 25) – as are various plants; Adam is told to "work" and "keep" the Garden (Genesis 2:15) – two words that only appear together elsewhere when referring to the priestly task of guarding the Temple (eg Numbers 3:7-8; 18:5-6). Above all, God is said to "walk" in Eden as he later "walks" among his people at his dwelling place, the Tabernacle (Leviticus 26:12; Deuteronomy 23:14).[29]

If the Garden was the place where Man enjoyed the presence of God it is not surprising to see some of its characteristics symbolised in the later Tabernacle and Temple, given their role.

The enduring significance of the Temple, as the place God enabled sinful man – once redeemed – to enjoy his presence, is

---

[29] For further exploration of the Garden functioning as a Temple, see T Desmond Alexander, *From Eden to the New Jerusalem*, (Nottingham: IVP, 2008), chapter 2. The most exhaustive study of this theme is found in G K Beale, *The Temple and the Church's Mission*, New Studies in Biblical Theology 17 (Leicester: Apollos, 2004). Something of a summary of Beale's treatment can be found in G K Beale, 'Eden, the Temple, and the Church's Mission in the New Creation', *Journal of the Evangelical Theological Society* 48/1 (March 2005).

apparent from the language of some of the Psalms (see, for example, Psalm 84, and the pilgrim Songs of Ascent, Psalms 120-134).

And yet, as we saw back in Chapter 5, after what might have been a wonderful conclusion following the establishment of Solomon's Temple, the Old Testament storyline undergoes major decline. Clearly, the earthly Temple in an earthly Jerusalem is not the last word on God's plan for his people to be in his presence. Once again, we are reminded there is a trajectory to be respected if we would understand Scripture correctly. So where is this element of the storyline heading?

We suggested that in the era after Solomon faith and hope were maintained through the medium of the writing prophets, who looked back on what God had done, in order to look forward to what God would do. This same principle can be applied to the concept of the Temple.

Ezekiel's book, for example, is written at the time of the Babylonian exile. Its early chapters depict idolatrous misuse of the Temple (Ezekiel 8) and the utterly devastating reality of the glory of the Lord departing (Ezekiel 10). It ends with a hope for the future that is expressed in terms of a glorious new Temple (Ezekiel 40-48).

The prophet Isaiah's book begins with a denunciation of Judah and its religious system – which, of course, was centred on the Temple (Isaiah 1). Isaiah then anticipates "the latter days" when the nations will come to "the mountain of the house of the Lord" (Isaiah 2).

Much of the first half of his book focuses on the Lord's judgement of his enemies, but the book concludes with a glorious hope for the future – expressed in terms of a new heavens and earth and a glorious future Jerusalem (Isaiah 60-66). As we have already noted, the significance of Jerusalem lay with the Temple. In between the earlier and latter parts of his book, Isaiah introduces us to the one who becomes the basis for that hope: the servant, who suffers on behalf of his people.

From our big-picture perspective we might say that the first Adam enjoyed God's presence in the Garden Temple – but was expelled after his rebellion. In the same way, Israel as God's son could experience God's presence at the Tabernacle and Jerusalem Temple – but was expelled after repeated rebellion and idolatry (the exile).

This pattern of failure fuels the anticipation and hope of the prophetic era, namely that God's promises would be fulfilled in a yet greater expression of all that the Temple stood for.

God's presence in the New Testament

In the final part of the Old Testament's storyline God brings his people back from exile. But although Jerusalem's Temple and walls are rebuilt, it all seems something of an anticlimax. The prophet Haggai appears to suggest that the rebuilt Temple doesn't even compare with Solomon's in terms of splendour (see Haggai 2:1-3): how much less, we might conclude, does it compare with the visionary hope of Ezekiel and Isaiah? But then we read:

> "For thus says the Lord of hosts: Yet once more, in a little while, I will shake the heavens and the earth and the sea and the dry land. And I will shake all nations, so that the treasures of all nations shall come in, and I will fill this house with glory, says the Lord of hosts. The silver is mine, and the gold is mine, declares the Lord of hosts. The latter glory of this house shall be greater than the former..." (Haggai 2:6-9)

And so, again, we see that perspective on which the Old Testament ends: there is more to come! This is as true of what the Temple stood for as it is of the promises made to Abraham and David. Moreover, the significance of the Temple is pointing in the same direction: it points to Jesus.

John's Gospel opens with a majestic prologue, which appears

deliberately to echo the opening words of Genesis: "In the beginning... was the Word..." (John 1:1). That prologue proclaims what we refer to as the Incarnation: the fullness of God being manifest in human form in the person of Jesus Christ. That proclamation reaches a resounding climax in John 1:14:

> "And the Word became flesh and *dwelt* among us, and we have seen his glory, glory as of the only Son from the Father, full of grace and truth." (John 1:14)

What John literally writes is that the Word "*tabernacled* among us". John's choice of verb is significant, and points his readers back to the Tabernacle, the place where God met with his people; the place where his presence was experienced. Jesus fulfils what the Tabernacle (and the later Temple) expressed: the presence of God among his people. This is brought out further in the next chapter of John:

> "So the Jews said to him, 'What sign do you show us for doing these things?' Jesus answered them, 'Destroy this temple, and in three days I will raise it up.' The Jews then said, 'It has taken forty-six years to build this temple, and will you raise it up in three days?' But he was speaking about the temple of his body."
> (John 2:18-21)

As the focus of God's presence, the Old Testament Tabernacle and Temple were also, necessarily, the place where sin was atoned for. Sinful Man cannot enter the presence of an utterly holy God unless sin is dealt with.

And so, of course, Jesus fulfils the sacrificial system of the Old Testament Temple in his once-for-all atoning death on the cross.

This facet of Jesus' mission, his coming and sacrificial death, has huge implications for the overall storyline of the Bible, as the New Testament demonstrates. The physical Temple in Jerusalem, both as a place where sin is atoned for, and where God's presence may then be enjoyed, is now redundant: Jesus has fulfilled all that the Temple expressed and, indeed, was pointing towards.

Furthermore, one of the consequences of being united to Jesus by faith – of being "in Christ", to use the apostle Paul's popular phrase – is that we, the church, become the Temple of God. This understanding of the church is expressed at various points in the New Testament (see, for example, 1 Corinthians 3:16; & 6:19; Ephesians 2:19-22). It is also, perhaps, an oft-neglected, and yet significant, aspect of the events that occur on the Day of Pentecost. In contrast to the kind of issues that tend to dominate Christians' studies of Acts 2, we ought to recognise a parallel between the disciples' experience and the glory of the Lord filling both the Tabernacle and Temple (which we referred to earlier, in Exodus 40:34-35 and 1 Kings 8:10-11). In the Old Testament God dwelt *among* his people – as his glory filled the Temple – now, Luke is signalling, he will dwell *within* his people – by his Holy Spirit. Luke's important quotation of the prophet Joel's promise (Joel 2:28-32 in Acts 2:17-21) seems to support this point.

In what is a very readable and succinct study, James Hamilton argues that in the Old Testament believers were *regenerate* (that is, born again) by the Spirit, but not *indwelt* by the Spirit – for God dwelt in the Temple. In the New Testament believers are both regenerate *and* indwelt by the Spirit – for we *are* the Temple.[30]

So we see that, as we observe the trajectory of the Bible's storyline, the theme of God's presence with his people starts in

---

[30] James M Hamilton Jr, *God's Indwelling Presence: The Holy Spirit in the Old and New Testaments* (Nashville: B&H Publishing, 2006)

the Garden. After the disastrous impact of Man's rebellion and fall into sin, God's provision for the restoration of his presence develops through the Tabernacle to the Temple to Jesus Christ. Through spiritual union with him, his people, the church, can now be identified as that temple.

A big-picture reading of Scripture prepares us to comprehend the magnitude and brilliance of John's final vision; a vision of what is yet to be fully revealed.

God's presence in the age to come

John writes: "And I heard a loud voice from the throne saying, 'Behold, the dwelling place ("tabernacle") of God is with man. He will dwell with them, and they will be his people, and God himself will be with them as their God" (Revelation 21:3).

In the Old Testament God's covenant with his people is frequently expressed in terms of the promise that he will be their God and they will be his people. Here we see the climax of that. The promise has become reality.

This thought is repeated – and arguably magnified – in the next chapter. It has been suggested that, in some ways, Revelation 22:4 is the most stunning verse in the whole Bible! John writes: "They will see his face..." Moses was told that man cannot see the face of God and live (Exodus 33:20). Even the seraphim of heaven are depicted as covering their faces before the holiness of God (Isaiah 6:2). John's vision is telling us that, at the final consummation of all things, when promise finally gives way to reality, we shall experience and enjoy the presence of God to the full!

Revelation 21 and 22 are chapters we should read and meditate on frequently. I've heard it said that Jonathan Edwards, the famous 18th-century American preacher-theologian, made it a practice to meditate on the new heavens and new earth every day. Such a perspective will inevitably shape the way we live. It will also shape how we respond to the things we have been considering in this book: the sufferings presently experienced as we live with the already-not-yet of God's promises.

Like any good ending to a good story, the Bible's final plot resolution sets everything that goes before in its proper context. As the apostle Paul wrote to the church in Rome: "For I consider that the sufferings of this present time are not worth comparing with the glory that is to be revealed to us" (Romans 8:18).

WHEN CONFLICT IS NO MORE

As we have journeyed through the storyline of the Bible, we have been focusing on God's promise and the conflict that is set against it. We have seen how that promise is expressed at key stages in the story, and how the general trajectory of Scripture points us to Jesus as the one who fulfils each expression of those promises. Crucially, even after the victory of his resurrection, we have seen that there is an 'already' and a 'not yet' to the fulfilment of promise in the gospel. Already Jesus has been victorious, but not yet has every knee bowed in acknowledgment that he is the rightful Lord of all.

All of this, as we suggested in the previous chapter, helps us both understand and respond appropriately, and biblically, to the harsh reality of the persecution of Christians today.

We have just observed the way in which John's final vision in the book of Revelation depicts the promise of God's presence becoming a reality. One day all that Jesus has accomplished, in fulfilling Old Testament promise, will be consummated and experienced fully.

It is fitting, and in keeping with the structure of all the chapters in Part Two of this book, to see what John also says about **conflict** at the end of all things.

John sees a new heaven and new earth, and yet he sees it as a new Jerusalem which, in turn, he sees as a temple, the full and final expression of what it means for God's people to experience the presence of God. Indeed, there is no temple – in the earthly sense – for God *is* the temple (Revelation 21:22), which seems to be another way of saying God is with his people.

As we have already noted earlier in this chapter, John's vision is suggestive of how the story began, back in the Garden. But now there is no prohibition on eating of the tree of life, for now God's people have entered, fully and finally, into the eternal presence of the Lord.

But there is something else that is absent.

John tells us: "No longer will there be anything *accursed...*" (Revelation 22:3). "Cursed are you," the Lord had said to the serpent (Genesis 3:14). "And now you are cursed," he said to Cain, whose actions identify him as a seed of the serpent (Genesis 4:11). "And him who dishonours you I will curse," the Lord declared in the midst of the promises he made to Abraham (Genesis 12:3).

At each key stage in the storyline, we have observed not only how promise is expressed at that point, but the fact that opposition to the promise continues. The world, behind which we see the serpent, continues to rail against God and his anointed one. Even after the life, death, resurrection and ascension of Jesus Christ, opposition continues as the apostles preach the gospel, in the already-not-yet age in which we live.

But now, here in Revelation 21 and 22, that opposition is no more. John has, of course, already depicted the final judgement on evil and the evil one in the preceding chapters of his book. As he concludes his final vision, of the glorious age to come, he considers it important to stress the implication of that final judgement: "No longer will there be anything accursed."

It seems that a similar point is being made at the beginning of this final vision. John began it thus: "Then I saw a new heaven and a new earth, for the first heaven and the first earth had passed away, *and the sea was no more*" (Revelation 21:1).

What's with this absence of sea?

I suspect that readers steeped in Old Testament imagery would have picked up the point. In the Old Testament the sea is sometimes depicted as a source of evil rebellion against God (see Job 26:12-13; Psalm 74:13-14; Isaiah 27:1). John has already deployed this imagery earlier in the book of Revelation (see 13:1).

All evil rebellion against God will have been removed: that's what John is saying. To rest in that assurance is not to gloat over the prospective future judgement of those who persecute us. As we suggested back in Chapter 4, as long as we live in this present life we are to pray for our persecutors, that God will bring them to repentance and faith – that God will bless them, too, in other words.

Nevertheless, we and all Christ's followers are to be reassured that our enjoyment of the eternal presence of God – our "reigning with him forever and ever" (Revelation 22:5) – will not be hampered, limited or disturbed by any opposition whatsoever. Then, and only then, the persecution of Christ's church will be a thing of the past.

OUR RESPONSE TO THE END OF THE STORY

So, what is our response to this final chapter of God's storyline? After a good ending to a good novel we may experience a certain sense of satisfaction. We have enjoyed the journey. We would probably recommend it to our friends, and we may well choose to read the story again at some point in the future.

Clearly God's storyline means so much more than that; that's why we encourage one another to read the Scriptures regularly! Here is God's truth, against which we measure all that we encounter in the course of this life. God's truth interprets our world, not vice versa. And the end of the story sets earlier elements of the story in proper context.

The visions that comprise John's book of Revelation declare God's sovereignty and Christ's Lordship – against the opposition that we continue to see in these in-between times. In his introduction John writes:

> "Behold, he is coming with the clouds, and every eye will see him, even those who pierced him, and all

tribes of the earth will wail on account of him. Even so. Amen." (Revelation 1:7)

The promise of the age to come – whenever it is articulated in the New Testament – is intended to shape the way we live our lives now. This should be no less true for the glorious vision of Revelation 21 & 22. The assurance that in that day there will no longer be anything accursed is followed by the declaration that God's "servants will worship him" (Revelation 22:3).

In the previous chapter we saw how, in the already-not-yet age in which we presently live, the strengthening of persecuted Christians and the encouraging of them to persevere in the faith is a fundamental response to the afflictions they experience. Part of that work of strengthening – a work of discipling – will be to enable Christians to see the big picture of Scripture, to understand not only what God has promised and fulfilled in Christ, but the relationship between the age in which we now live, and the age to come.[31]

Maintaining this perspective is for our encouragement, and for the encouragement of all God's people.

> "Blessed are those who wash their robes, so that they may have the right to the tree of life and that they may enter the city by the gates." (Revelation 22:14)

> "He who testifies to these things says, 'Surely I am coming soon.' Amen. Come, Lord Jesus!" (Revelation 22:20)

---

[31] A relationship that is distorted by purveyors of the so-called 'prosperity gospel'

Conclusion:
The Discoveries of the Journey

PERSECUTION is not a theme Christians can avoid. The information-heavy age in which we live means that we are quickly and easily made aware of what is happening to fellow believers in Christ around the world today.

Those of us living in cultures that have long enjoyed religious freedom may be appalled by what we hear and read and, moreover, may struggle to come to terms with what we know our fellow Christians are experiencing. Stories of persecution can be both distressing and discouraging. And yet when we turn to the Bible we discover that opposition and hostility is commonplace. In the New Testament age, Christians were taught that such opposition is the norm: it is to be expected.

And so it is to the Bible that we have turned in this brief study, to help us understand persecution and to see how as Christians we should respond. To do this we have adopted what we have called a big-picture, biblical theology approach to reading the Bible, believing this is how the Bible teaches us to read the Bible. In particular, we have concentrated on the theme of God's promise, as it develops through the Bible's storyline, to its fulfilment in Jesus Christ.

Promise and conflict

In fact, as we have done so we have seen, at each turning point in the Bible's story, how God's expression of promise at that point in the story can be tracked through the bigger storyline to Christ and the gospel. He is the individual seed of the woman who will conquer the serpent and his seed – but not without suffering himself; he is the individual descendant of Abraham, through whom all kinds of people will be blessed by God; he is the son of David, who will establish a kingdom of peace for ever.

At the same time, we have observed that at each turning point conflict is present. This conflict is the response of those who reject God and his promises, who rebel against him. This conflict helps us understand the origin and inevitability of persecution in this present age.

Christ's incarnation, life, death and resurrection fulfilled every facet of the promises God had made to restore his Creation. And yet, two thousand years on, evil is still present in our world; conflict is still with us. Christ's people continue to suffer persecution.

The reason for this is the already-not-yet tension that is present in the New Testament; something the first followers of Jesus had to get their heads round. Christ's resurrection – his victory – did not mean the End had come all at once. Jesus himself had proclaimed that the kingdom had come – and yet was still to come. As he faced the prospect of the cross, Jesus could declare: "Now is the judgement of this world; now will the ruler of this world be cast out" (John 12:31). And yet, the night before he was crucified he warned his disciples: "If they persecuted me, they will also persecute you" (John 15:20).

It is so important that we grasp both aspects of this already-not-yet of the Bible's story. If we fail to grasp the 'already', we may come to doubt the absolute certainty of Christ's victory and the victory we have in him. If we fail to grasp the 'not yet', we may begin to find the realities of suffering and persecution overwhelming and faith-destroying. The ground we covered in Chapter 7 is so important in this respect.

So what have we discovered as we have journeyed through the Bible's story?

Promise and persecution

We began with the first promise, a promise in the midst of judgement, in fact, in Genesis 3:15. As God spoke words of judgement to the serpent, his words offered hope to the man and woman of a future. Of victory in the end. Although they had been duped and led astray by the serpent's wiles, a seed of the woman would one day strike a decisive blow, even though assaulted by the serpent himself. This Christ does at the cross.

But this promise spoke of an enduring enmity between the woman and the serpent, and between their respective seed. As the story unfolds we see people being identified either as seed of the woman or seed of the serpent: God's people or God's enemies. We hesitate to see the world around us in such black-and-white terms but, spiritually, this is the reality.

This first expression of God's promise shows us the spiritual root behind everything that leads to the persecution of Christians. At the same time, we see God's assurance of final victory.

In that certainty we should encourage every Christian to live.

In Genesis 12 we saw God calling Abraham. God's promise is now expressed in terms of blessing. In particular, God is going to bless all kinds of people through Abraham and his line. Ultimately, as the New Testament interprets it, this points us to Christ and the gospel.

And yet, in the midst of this promise, Abraham is reminded that there are those who will dishonour the one who brings God's blessing. These God will curse: an expression of judgement first spoken against the serpent. Chilling and serious though this threat is, it is God alone who executes it. The Bible's subsequent testimony is that we leave such final judgement to God. In the meantime, as long as both we and those who dishonour Christ are living in this life, we are to seek to be channels of God's blessing: offering Christ in the gospel to everyone – even our most strident opponents.

As God's promise expands, then, we are reminded that a biblical response to a biblical understanding of persecution will include a desire to respond to hatred with love: to go on offering Christ even to those who, in the very act of persecuting Christians, are demonstrating their rejection of Christ.

One of the key factors to emerge in Chapter 5, when we considered God's covenant with David, is the shape of the storyline itself. With the Promised Land entered, everything seems to be heading for a natural climax. God's glorious presence in Solomon's temple (1 Kings 8:10,11) and Solomon's declaration that God had kept all his promises (1 Kings 8:56) seems to endorse this.

And yet this apparent plot resolution proves not to be the end. Instead, we see a decline in the faith and fortunes of God's people that results eventually in exile. As Adam had been exiled from God's presence in the Garden, so Israel is exiled from God's presence in the Temple.

So marked is this decline that we might be tempted to question the value of God's promises. The experience of persecution, or the observing of others suffering persecution, can have the same effect today.

The response to this perplexity comes from the prophets and the psalmists. Understanding, as they do, their history (or rather God's history!), they use imagery and elements from the Abraham-to-David storyline to look forward to a yet greater work God will do to truly fulfil all of his promises.

Once again, this epoch in the big picture points us to Christ and the gospel. He accomplishes a greater saving work than was seen at the Exodus. He will establish a kingdom that will truly and fully restore God's creation purposes.

And so this part of the story reminds us that true biblical faith is forward-looking. Our hope, ultimately, is not for this life, but for the promised Messianic kingdom when it comes in all its fullness. The prophets and psalmists encourage us to focus on what is still to come. This hope is what sustains us, even in the midst of persecution.

When we turn from the Old Testament, with its note of 'more still to come', into the New Testament we quickly find Jesus being presented as the one in whom all of God's promises are indeed fulfilled. He is the true son of David and descendant of Abraham.

And yet conflict is still present. Jesus experiences it at the beginning of his life – and it is still there at the end of his life. The seed of the serpent is still bruising the seed of the woman. The Gospels end with the triumphant resurrection of Jesus and the charge to go and proclaim the gospel to the world. But the end has not yet come! Jesus' victory is, in a strange way, a victory before the end. Here, again, we see the tension with which we live, as we await his return. How does this help us understand, and respond to, persecution?

As we live in these in-between times, Christians are caught up in a spiritual battle. Satan is a defeated foe – but a defiant foe, who continues to make war on the corporate seed of the woman. One of the ways he does this is through persecution. We need to understand this – but also to remember that in Christ we do already have the victory!

This already-not-yet tension becomes one of the key themes in the book of Acts. Luke's second volume emphasises that the last days – the period between Christ's coming and his coming again – will be characterised by gospel preaching and the spread of God's word, but *also* by opposition to that gospel from the world. We should expect to see both happening, although not necessarily in a uniform, consistent way at every point in time. In Christ's resurrection the age to come has broken into this present age. However, we still await the final consummation of the promises that Christ has fulfilled. It was at this point, in reviewing the apostle Paul's first missionary journey and later writings, that we observed strong pointers to our response to the persecution of Christians.

The already-not-yet dimensions of the age in which we live make paramount the task of strengthening Christians and encouraging them to persevere in the faith – particularly in the face of the world's opposition and persecution. This discipling is done with a prayerful dependence on the Lord.

Discipleship is fundamental to the life of the church. Such discipleship must include space to address the reality, inevitability and meaning of opposition and persecution.

In Chapter 8 we reached the end of the story – and the end of the age in which we live. The final, glorious vision of the Bible is of the new heaven and new earth. Here God's people enjoy his presence to the full. Evil, conflict and persecution are no more.

Here we were reminded that part of the task of discipling is to enable Christians to see the big picture of Scripture, to understand not only what God has promised and fulfilled in Christ, but also the relationship between the age in which we now live and the age to come.

Implications

So, finally, what are the implications of the things we have discovered? What does a big-picture, biblical theology approach to the issue of persecution imply, in terms of how the church of Jesus Christ is to respond? What are the important principles that we need to keep hold of? Let me suggest five, as we close.

1. The spiritual significance of the persecution of Christians

It is vital that we develop and maintain a biblical understanding and definition of the persecution of God's people. A biblical understanding will equip us to make a biblical response.

Christians are not, of course, the only people in this world to suffer persecution, to be ill-treated because of who they are.

Within recent history we have seen awful examples of so-called ethnic or tribal cleansing in different parts of the world. Christians are not even the only people in this world to suffer persecution for what we might refer to as 'religious reasons'.

Nevertheless, in terms of the big picture – God's big story – the persecution of Christians *is* unique *spiritually*.

All persecution is wrong, of course. All persecution manifests and illustrates the general sinfulness of mankind. "Man's inhumanity to man" is but one illustration of the sinfulness and evil of the human heart, which needs the redemption and cleansing of Christ's atoning sacrifice.

But the persecution of Christians is ultimately, and spiritually, unique. This is not because the physical aspects are necessarily more severe: it is because of the significance it has within redemption history, within the big picture. The persecution of Christians evidences the one division within mankind that has eternal significance. It is part of the conflict between the seed of the woman and the seed of the serpent.

2. *The need to teach a biblical theology of persecution*

This follows from the point just made. If I accidentally cut my hand in the kitchen, it may be sufficient to apply a plaster, until the cut heals. However, if, on another occasion, I start to develop a serious and painful rash on my hand, a plaster is not going to solve it. At best it may prevent me scratching the rash. But I need to get to the bottom of what's causing the rash in the first place and address that.

That may not be a great analogy, but I hope you get the point. We need a biblical understanding of persecution, and its significance within the big picture of God's story, to help us respond correctly, to frame a biblical response that is in accord with God's purposes.

When the church is called to respond to the persecution of Christians, it is not simply being called to make an emotional response to a humanitarian injustice. The persecution of

Christians certainly *is* an injustice, of course – but it is so much more. We must never allow ourselves to see the persecution of Christians as merely a human rights issue. Everything we have observed during our journey through the Bible tells us it is much more than that.

3. The priority of discipleship

That response must begin with the discipleship of God's people. After all, in his final great commission, Jesus did not tell his disciples just to 'preach for a conversion'; he told them to make disciples and to teach those disciples how to live (Matthew 28:19-20).

We saw in Chapter 7 how the apostle Paul responded when he knew other Christians were being persecuted. He set out to *strengthen* them and to *encourage them to persevere* in their faith. This task of strengthening the church becomes a significant theme in the book of Acts and is, arguably, the main reason for the New Testament letters!

The apostle Peter's first letter is a fine example of this priority. Writing to Christians who were facing hostility from a world that was opposed to Christ, Peter writes to urge them to stand firm in the true grace of God (1 Peter 5:12).[32]

4. The need to ensure the persecuted are taught God's big-picture truth

In a moving farewell speech to Christians in Ephesus, and in a context where he emphasises the reality of opposition to gospel ministry, Paul could declare of his time with God's people: "I did not shrink from declaring to you the whole counsel of God" (Acts 20:27).

It may sound patronising to talk of teaching the persecuted about persecution. But is that not what the apostle Paul did, in the various places he visited?

Just because Christians have suffered severely for Christ –

---

[32] For further reflection on 1 Peter, see Kenneth Harrod, *Jars of Clay*, pp.98-105

and just because, by God's undoubted grace, they have persevered thus far, in the face of that persecution – does not necessarily mean they have a full biblical grasp of why that persecution has occurred or how they, and others around them, are to respond and go on responding.

The reality is that persecuted Christians are often living in situations where they have been starved of solid, big-picture biblical teaching. But the church of God always needs to be taught the word of God. That's why God gives to the church pastor-teachers.

Of course we need to feed and clothe those who have suffered, and to help them rebuild homes and churches that have been burned down, and to provide essential medical care when they have been brutally assaulted or tortured. There are times when it will be right to speak out about the plight of the persecuted and to campaign on their behalf. But we fall short if we neglect their discipleship, and if we fail to resource them biblically.

5. *Remembering that we have a message of hope*

As we said at the start of this concluding chapter, persecution can be a distressing and discouraging topic to think about. Some Christians simply don't want to hear about it.

We certainly need to be made aware of what is happening to our fellow Christians around the world. We need vehicles of communication to be informed (not least to fuel our intercessory prayer). But in telling the *stories*, we must never lose sight of *the story*. We must never lose sight of the big picture that God gives us in the Scriptures. As we said in Chapter 8, God's truth interprets our world, not vice versa. We know the end of the story. We know the direction in which God's great plan and purpose for the whole of Creation is heading. We know why persecution will occur until Christ returns.

A biblical appreciation of the big picture – the reading and understanding of what we have called God's story – reminds every Christian that ultimately we are truly more than conquerors through him who loved us. Ultimately, we can be assured, nothing in all of creation can separate us from the love of God that is ours in Christ Jesus our Lord (Romans 8:37-39).

We began the central part of this book by reflecting on the meaning and significance of that first promise-in-judgement of Genesis 3:15. We saw how it pointed to an individual seed of the woman who would conquer the serpent and his seed.

At the same time, we have referred, on several occasions during the course of this book, to the important relationship between the corporate group and the individual representative. 'In Christ' we are the corporate seed of the woman.

We close observing the apostle Paul's appreciation of that important relationship. In what is a clear allusion to Genesis 3:15, Paul declares to the collective group of Christians in Rome:

> "The God of peace will soon crush Satan under your feet. The grace of our Lord Jesus Christ be with you."
> (Romans 16:20)

Appendix:
Further reading on biblical theology

IN Part One of this book, I argued for what I have been calling a big-picture, biblical theology reading of the Scriptures. This, I believe, is how the Bible teaches us to read the Bible.

The risen Lord Jesus taught his first disciples to see a trajectory in the Scriptures that finds its fulfilment – and therefore its ultimate meaning – in him.

Although not the main theme of this book, Chapter 2 provided important tools to enable us to follow the Bible's storyline and to address what *has* been the book's main theme: developing a biblical understanding of the persecution of Christians, and of how we should respond to that persecution.

Understanding and being able to follow the plot of any good story is not only necessary – it is rewarding! It is satisfying. And so, for the Christian, biblical theology is exciting, and rewarding. To see the big picture is to hear God and to understand better his promises and his purposes.

If you wish to explore a biblical theological reading of Scripture further, here are some suggestions:

Introductory reading
What is Biblical Theology?
James M Hamilton Jr (Wheaton: Crossway, 2014)
Hamilton has a sharp theological mind, and a wonderful writer's pen. He's not afraid of using two-word sentences to drive home a point. In barely 116 pages, he introduces us to the Bible's big story, and its use of imagery and types. A great place to start.

According to Plan
Graeme Goldsworthy (Leicester; IVP, 1991)
Goldsworthy served a previous generation of Christians with his concise, clear writing in a similar way to Hamilton. In the 1980s he wrote several very brief books on different parts of Scripture. In *According to Plan* he covers the whole Bible, with very readable, short chapters, enhanced by useful tables. Each ends with a study guide, making it a superb book to use in small groups for those who want a better grasp of the big picture of Scripture.

From Eden to the New Jerusalem
T Desmond Alexander (Nottingham: IVP, 2008)
Alexander's approach to understanding God's big story is to start at the end – in Revelation 21 and 22. He then addresses the big story thematically, tackling in turn: the presence of God, the sovereignty of God, the defeat of evil, redemption, life and hope. Much valuable ground is covered, effectively and clearly, in less than 200 pages.

Further reading

Biblical Theology in the Life of the Church
Michael Lawrence (Wheaton: Crossway, 2010)
A very helpful book for anyone involved in teaching God's word. Lawrence considers first the tools for doing so, and is really clear and helpful on the relationship between biblical theology and systematic theology. He then goes on to consider some of the big themes of the Bible.

Preaching the whole Bible as Christian Scripture
Graeme Goldsworthy (Leicester: IVP, 2000)
Goldsworthy's books that have followed *According to Plan* (see above) have tended, on the whole, to be bigger reads. This is one of the most helpful. In Part One he provides a thorough introduction to biblical theology. In Part Two he applies these principles to the various genres of Scripture.

Walking with Jesus through his Word
Dennis E Johnson (Phillipsburg: P&R Publishing, 2015)
Johnson starts with the teaching of Jesus in Luke 24. From this vantage point, he walks us through the Bible addressing, along the way, the importance of context, the use of types in the story, the covenant shape of Scripture's story, and the various ways in which Jesus fulfils earlier Scriptural episodes, characters and roles. He offers many wonderful examples of a biblical theology approach to the Bible.

Essential reading

What's the best book for learning about biblical theology? The Bible! Lest you think I'm stating the obvious, what I mean, of course, is the development of a big-picture reading of that Bible.

Find a programme that helps you read the Bible in a year, for example – and preferably one that provides one longer reading per day, rather than several shorter ones that jump around. See this not as a one-off challenge for next year, but as the way you want to go on reading God's word on a regular basis. Getting used to reading the Bible in big chunks is the best way to start to appreciate the shape of the story – and, therefore, the message of the story and of its various parts.

Also by Kenneth Harrod:

Jars of Clay clearly reminds us that persecution is at the centre of our Christian faith. The book gives a clear biblical perspective on persecution, and includes details of some of the persecuted believers from around the world whom the author has met as part of his ministry with Release. The book focuses on five key areas: mission, the gospel, grace, the church and hope. Each chapter concludes with a number of questions for personal reflection or discussion, making it ideal for use in a Bible study or home group or as the basis for a teaching series within your church.
£8.00 inc p&p to UK addresses.

Available from www.releaseinternational.org/books
Or by calling our Supporter Relations Team on 01689 823491.

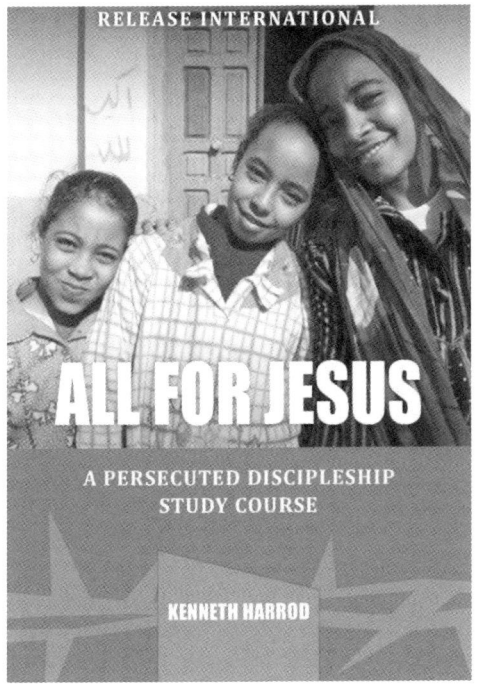

All for Jesus is a small group Bible study series that enables us to get to grips with Christian discipleship in a world that is hostile to Jesus. The five studies have been written by Kenneth Harrod. Each study focuses on a passage of Scripture, with introductory notes and questions. There are helpful notes for groups leaders at the back.
£4.00 for one or £9.00 for ten inc p&p.

Available from www.releaseinternational.org/books
Or by calling our Supporter Relations Team on 01689 823491.